What Others Are Saying about Esther Wildenberg and This Book

"Esther Wildenberg is a living example that being undermined can fuel you to tap into your divine power, thereby getting to know your true identity as an individual so you can start living your life on your terms. *The Undermined Soul* is a must read for every human who wants to restart their life and live it to the fullest with dreams, vision, and making a greater difference in the world. The power is yours."

— **Kathy Buckley, Comedian, Author, and Motivational Speaker**

"Esther shows you how you don't need to step into your pants—you need to step into your power!"

— **Jeffrey Gitomer, King of Sales, Best-Selling Author, International Keynote Speaker, and Sales Strategist**

"I've been to five of Esther Wildenberg's Mastermind Retreats. With each retreat, I leave refreshed, invigorated, and restored to go back into my life with energy and clarity to positively influence my family, business, and community. Taking the time to attend Esther's retreats is an investment in myself, which allows me to contribute to others more effectively."

— **Teresa Ryan, Century 21**

"Esther is a very pleasant, professional person to work with and is focused on delivering results."

— **Michael van Den Berg, Head of Audit, Shell Global**

"I met Esther in a dynamic phase in a changing organization. She has the ability to combine creative thoughts with a results-driven approach. As a business consultant, she perfectly keeps the balance between the interests of businesses and individuals. What most struck me is her never-ceasing positivism, making her always capable of finding a solution and seeing the sunny side!"

— **Annet Luijendijk, Executive Consultant ING**

"Esther is a very dedicated and committed professional with a strong focus on results and customer satisfaction."

— **Jeroen Aalbers, Advisor and Board Member of Fortune 1000 Companies**

"Esther helped our team get to know each other in our first global face-to-face team meeting after COVID by implanting the BANK methodology into our department."

— **Johan Storm, Supply Chain Lead Offshore Wind, Shell Global**

"Esther is a soulful and inspirational thought-leader, communication expert, and entrepreneur. She is a powerful influencer who pours into those she serves at the highest level and doesn't hold back. She empowers all those around her to rise, be the best versions of themselves, and take action that affects change. As a mastermind facilitator and an international speaker, Esther shares from her heart, and her stories never fail to touch yours. She is dynamic, vulnerable, and unapologetically authentic. I recommend connecting with and having a conversation with Esther. Your business (and life) will thank you."

— **Patty Farmer, Marketing, Media, and Money Expert, Speaker, Podcast Host, and Business Growth Strategist**

"Before Esther Wildenberg and I met in person, she already knew my personality type. As the cofounder of Codebreaker Technologies and an expert in personality types, she can evaluate your personality in nanoseconds; she won the contract with my company because of that skill. Having dealt with Esther for the past few years, I know she is passionate about her work; she is also exceptionally kind to deal with, and in the corporate world, that is hard to come by nowadays. She is thoughtful, supportive, and energetic when she works on a project. I vouch for Esther Wildenberg as an organizational consultant and an event speaker for both personal and business development."

— **Belynda Lee, MBA, COO, and Author**

"I have worked with Esther in multiple capacities, but primarily, she has served as a coach to me. Her strengths include speaking truths you want to ignore while making it safe for you to finally acknowledge them. If you ever have the chance to attend a retreat with Esther, do it. She has been instrumental in helping me transition from a military officer to an entrepreneur; she can help you make whatever transition you are trying to make. She is a powerful salesperson and sales trainer with an international perspective that we frequently lack in the United States. I wish I had found her sooner."

— **Jennifer Draper, Financial Coach**

"Esther strikes me as a professional who knows how to serve the customer accordingly. Creative solutions for complex problems."

— **Klaas de Groot, Chain Director, Europe**

"I have experienced Esther as a committed worker. She focuses on her goals. As a people manager, she gives her staff a lot of possibilities for growth and tries to give her passion to everyone. She's a high-skilled, professional, and warm person. Since we met, Esther has shown a great passion for any project she takes on and is very reliable about finishing it as promised."

— **Lisette van Geelen, Event Manager, NKC Europe**

"I have had the pleasure of knowing Esther Wildenberg for the past several years. She did not fail me a single time. Esther is a highly organized person with very strong problem-solving skills. An experienced perfectionist and insightful partner, she constantly shows a lot of analytical capability and a willingness to advance both her personal and professional development."

— **Thomas Delbarge, Planet IT BeNeLux**

"I have had the honor and pleasure of attending several of Esther Wildenberg's mastermind and training events, including, most recently, an amazing event in Costa Rica. She's a 'mastermind master.' Esther excels in designing her masterminds around deep experience, starting each day with meditation and focusing on positive transformation. She carefully creates content specific to her audience's needs and creates experiential learning through targeted, thought-provoking exercises. As a skilled facilitator, Esther is intuitively attentive to her group's learning and engagement in the content and experience. I look forward to more events with Esther!"

— **Laurel Rolls, Certified Executive/Professional Coach ICF**

"Thanks to Esther Wildenberg, cofounder of Codebreaker Technologies, I went from $265,000 annual income to more than $1,000,000 in gross commissions in six years. Codebreaker Technologies and the BANK system has been a major factor in helping me achieve my sales success. Since taking the course in 2015, I have been able to understand my clients' needs more easily, appreciate my clients' values, and communicate so much more effectively so that people feel understood and heard. This higher emotional intelligence has generated such a high level of trust between me and my clients that they hire me again and again and recommend me to their friends. I know I would not be where I am now without the Codebreaker technology in my sales toolkit."

— **Jane Johnston, REMAX, Victoria, British Columbia**

"Retreats with Esther Wildenberg are a game-changer, seamlessly blending powerful information with soulful self-discovery. Having attended several retreats with her, I know you'll discover a transformative experience that unlocks your full potential, offering practical tools and personalized strategies to align your mindset and soul set. Guided by her passion, Esther empowers you to confidently face any challenge. The retreat's holistic approach and supportive community make it a must-attend for those ready to level up their lives and work toward self-mastery."

— **Eric Goodman, PhD, Certified Business Coach, Consultant, and Trainer, Meridian Success Group**

"Esther is a speaker who will light the fire of inspiration and challenge you to commit to change. She does not dance around the challenges we all face on our success journey, and her honesty is what allows people to take steps forward."

— **Jaime Taets, CEO of Keystone Group International**

"Esther, you are an extraordinarily gifted and inspirational speaker. Your level of connection and clarity with the audience brought back memories of Walter Cronkite and Walt Disney. Thank you for your contribution to our leadership event. You created a buzz!"

— **Nick Ryan, Executive Chairman, Marquette Companies**

"Esther Wildenberg's retreat is an absolute game-changer! It was an experience that propelled me to new heights. Right from the get-go, Esther's dynamic energy and compelling vision for personal growth set the stage for an unparalleled journey. Her retreats are not just retreats; they are transformative experiences designed to deliver immediate and substantial results. Esther's compassion and dedication to making a difference are deeply felt, and it's clear she truly cares about everyone's journey and seeing them reach their full potential! I wholeheartedly recommend Esther Wildenberg's retreats to anyone looking to make a significant difference in their life. The experience is fast-paced, supportive, and gets you real results. Don't miss the opportunity to be part of something iconic!"

— **Michelle Lee, Business Coaching LLC**

"Esther Wildenberg is not just an exceptional leadership speaker—she's a true catalyst for empowerment during her retreats and masterminds because they're transformational!"

— **Lisa Thomas, Epigenetics for Global Impact**

"Attending the RISE Retreat was truly a beautiful, empowering, and transformative experience. From the moment I arrived, I felt welcomed and connected. The thoughtfully curated activities allowed me to explore my inner self, release what no longer served me, and manifest my desires. I left feeling rejuvenated, inspired, and armed with tools to navigate my journey ahead. The connections I made with fellow participants were genuinely uplifting, creating a sense of community I will cherish forever. I am so grateful to Esther and her team for crafting such a magical experience that touched my heart and soul. If you're seeking growth and empowerment, I can't recommend a RISE Retreat enough!"

— **Mariana Bayramyan, The Conscious Hairstylist**

"The RISE Retreat with Esther was a transformative experience that moved my personal life and professional growth forward. Esther's charismatic and dynamic approach was insightful. She gave us practical strategies to work on immediately. I normally do not show or share my feelings or emotions, but this retreat had me digging deeper than I ever had before. Esther pushed me out of my comfort zone, which opened my heart and mind to new ways of looking at things. The retreat provided an exclusive setting with other professionals who were also eager to make significant improvements in their journey. It fostered an atmosphere of encouragement and trust, which enriched the experience. Through Esther's guidance, we learned to harness our energy and channel it toward achieving our goals and dreams, even after leaving the retreat."

— **Gladys Boutwell, Employee Benefits Consultant**

"In *The Undermined Soul*, Esther Wildenberg shares her incredible journey from letting others steal her power to becoming a dynamic entrepreneur and a beautiful human being. She is living proof that you can create your own destiny when you listen to your internal guidance system rather than the negative voices that surround you. Her positive outlook on life, fueled by her international experiences, will make you better appreciate your world and be eager to explore all the other worlds still out there waiting for you."

— **Patrick Snow, Publishing Coach and International Bestselling Author of** *Creating Your Own Destiny* **and** *The Affluent Entrepreneur*

"I loved Esther's story of growing up in the Netherlands, becoming a business leader, and then taking the leap of faith to move to the United States where she married, had a child, and reinvented herself. In *The Undermined Soul*, she shares all the obstacles that tried to undermine her throughout her life, but her ability to overcome each one will inspire you to believe all good things are also possible for you—and then to make those good things your reality."

— **Tyler R. Tichelaar, PhD and Award-Winning Author of** *The Mysteries of Marquette*

YOUR TRANSFORMATION BLUEPRINT TO
BECOME AN EMPOWERED LEADER

THE UNDERMINED SOUL

Leadership Strategies to
Reveal Your Full Potential

ESTHER WILDENBERG

THE UNDERMINED SOUL
Leadership Strategies to Reveal Your Full Potential

Copyright © 2025 by Esther Wildenberg. All rights reserved.

Print version published by:
Aviva Publishing
Lake Placid, New York

Digital version published by:
Integrity Publishing International
Houston, Texas

All Rights Reserved. No part of this book may be used or reproduced in any manner whatsoever without the express written permission of the author.

Address all inquiries to:
Esther Wildenberg
+1 (858) 847-8368
Esther@EstherWildenberg.com
www.TheUnderminedSoul.com
www.EstherWildenberg.com

ISBN: 978-1-63618-386-2
Library of Congress Control Number: 2025906694

Editing: Superior Book Productions
Cover Design and Interior Book Layout: Fusion Creative Works
Author Photo: Janet Becker

Every attempt has been made to properly source all quotes.

Printed in the United States of America

Dedication

A special dedication to my son, Kai Keanu. He will probably never read this book; most kids don't read their parents' journals and books. However, I hope I inspire him by writing this book. My wish for him is to become an incredible human being who inspires many around the world with his leadership and his divine path in this lifetime.

I also dedicate this book to my wife and best friend, Cheri Tree. Over the past decade, she encouraged me to speak on stage and share my personal message. She has given me life experiences and business opportunities. I would have never reached my true potential without her support and love for me.

I also dedicate this book to every human I have connected with around the world in this lifetime, from conception until today and into the future. The moment you touch someone, hug them, or give them a handshake, you're connected for life. We're all one, and you have had an influence on me from maybe seconds up to decades.

Finally, I dedicate this book to *you*, the reader. May this book help you become an empowered leader and no longer be an undermined soul.

Acknowledgments

John Angiolillo, Michelle Myrter Angiolillo, Alfredo Bala, Michael Besson, Rich Boyer, Andy Broadaway, Kim Marie Branch-Pettid, Kathy Buckley, Stephanie Burton, Pasha Carter, Veronica Chew, Sarah Clayton, Winn Claybaugh, Michael Shaun Conaway, Angie Cross, Dawn Dahlby, Wendy Darling, Gabriella de Leeuw, Truus Druyts, Reggie Flowers, Talia Fox, Ron Gabaldon, Randy Garn, Laura Gisborne, Jeffrey Gitomer, Mary Glorfield, Christian Godon, Lisa Faeder Grossman, Dr. Aaron Gumm, Josselyne Herman-Saccio, Rich Higbee, Joshua Higgenbotham, Jennifer Hill, Marlon Holden, Mark Johnson, Hans Keirstead, Martha Krejci, Al Kwong, Loren Lahav, Belynda Lee, Dr. Jeff Magee, Lorene Martel, Yolanda Martinez, Jason McClain, Art McCracken, Garrett McGrath, Phil Michaels, Danny Morel, Dini Noorlander, Ted Nuyten, Alex Palacios, Christine Pannebakker, Mark Porteous, Armand Puyolt, Satyen Raya, Vera Renema, Forbes Riley, Steve Rodgers, Karin Rose, Nick Ryan, Teresa Ryan, Wendy Salyers, Sheri Sharman, Michael Silvers, Patrick Snow, Per van Spall, Julie Stephens, Jaime Taets, Kelley Tenny, Lisa Thomas, Cheri Tree, Jason Tyne, Michael van den Berg, Nicole van Leeuwen, Marcel Verkoijen, Mieke Verschoor, Rose Vitale, Denis Waitley, Michelle Wallach, Sandra Yancey, Jared Yellin, and Mark Yuzuik.

Contents

Preface: A Note to the Reader — 17

Introduction: Your Empowered Life Awaits — 23

Chapter 1: Undermined No More! — 27

Chapter 2: Unleashing the Tiger — 41

Chapter 3: Manifesting Abundance — 53

Chapter 4: Embracing Your Voice — 63

Chapter 5: Climbing the Mountain — 75

Chapter 6: Your Divine Right — 87

Chapter 7: Be a World Traveler — 97

Chapter 8: Deepen Your Leadership — 111

Chapter 9: Healing Your Life — 123

Chapter 10: Rocking the Boat — 135

Chapter 11: Life-Changing Routines — 149

Chapter 12: Near-Death Experience — 163

Chapter 13: Let Go. Forgive. Surrender. — 175

Chapter 14: Find Your Tribe	187
Chapter 15: Don't Die	199
Chapter 16: Circle of Influence	209
Chapter 17: Your Identity	223
Chapter 18: Create a Legacy	237
A Final Note: Become an Empowered Leader	249
About the Author	251
About Esther Wildenberg's Retreats and Mastermind Gatherings	253
About Codebreaker Technologies	257
Engage Esther Wildenberg as a Coach or Consultant	261
Book Esther Wildenberg to Speak at Your Next Event	265

Preface :
A Note to the Reader

I'm writing this book for very personal reasons. I realize your legacy only really happens when you're alive and able to influence other lives. It was fueled by my four-year-old son Kai asking me if we could read my book one night before he went to bed. I replied, "I have not written my book yet." It reminded me of the vows I wrote for him the day he was born (see Chapter 17). For many years, people have asked me when I will publish my book. "When it's the right time," has been my answer, and the time is now.

In our most private, silent moments, we pivot and connect with our true selves. We can change ourselves; we can change the world. We're spiritual beings having a human experience, and we're born with incredible potential. After working with one of my mentors, I realized how much of my potential I had left untapped my whole life. Each missed opportunity hurt me, but it inspired me to show the world what's possible and to love myself enough to live up to my highest potential, serving humanity and being an example for my son and followers.

Writing this book has made me a better human. This book was written during difficult times in the world, our business, my health, and our marriage. This book is drawn from my personal life, my ideas around leadership and spirituality, my two near-death experiences, my connection to Source, my twenty-five years' experience working with people, my mentors, coaches, and peers, and lastly, my general observations of the world. I wrote every word myself without using AI or a ghost writer. It has been a divine project twenty-five years in the making.

Everyone thinks Esther is living the dream, got lucky, and has had no challenges. Maybe on the outside it all looks like a fairytale and a lifestyle most people won't get to live. However, my life has not been one of pink clouds and rainbows. I have faced many challenges throughout my life to date. Life doesn't happen to us; it happens for us. In this book, I'm sharing the tip of the iceberg; there's so much more. Our daily experiences, setbacks, failures, mistakes, and fears teach us the daily life lessons we're here to learn. I have made millions, and I have lost millions. I have loved deeply and been heartbroken many times. I hid my true self for decades. I lived from paycheck to paycheck. I have been scared and depressed and felt I was worth nothing. I have been fired and rejected. I have been betrayed, undermined, underestimated, cheated on, and lied to. I have lost friends and family members. I have lost people I deeply loved out of jealousy.

In short, I can relate to you and your life story. And I want to encourage you to read this book with an open mind and heart. I want to thank you in advance for having the courage and making the time to read this book. All I wish for you is to become the person inside you who is waiting to be fully expressed. You're a brilliant soul who came to this planet to make a difference, small or big.

I want to thank my wife, Cheri Tree, for believing in me during our ten-year marriage with its ups and downs and showing me the way to become a speaker, leader, and author. I would like to express gratitude to my mentors, friends, and ex-partners. They all have a very special place in my heart. I want to thank all the people in my life who undermined me; you were the fuel to my drive, passion, resilience, compassion, and never-quit mentality. A very special thank you to the following people who were part of pivotable moments in my life: my dysfunctional but loving family; my first wife Mieke; my employer and mentor Vera; my coach Nicole; my ex-partner Manuella; my ex-partner and friend Truus, and her life partner and inspiration for writing my book, Christine; my thirty-five-year, rock-solid friend Stephanie; my dear friend and Kai's godmother, Angie; my beloved friends all over the world; my clients; my community members; my followers; the readers of this book; and my deepest inspiration, my son Kai, the "Emperor!"

"I prefer a woman who is unskillful, who is an awkward writer, but who has something to say, who is dealing with herself one time on every page."

— Ralph Keyes, *The Courage to Write*

"Everyone talks about how hard it is to trust people after you've been hurt, but barely anyone talks about how hard it is to trust yourself when you've had your gut instincts, dreams, plans, passion, and convictions skillfully undermined by someone."

— Esther Wildenberg

Introduction: Your Empowered Life Awaits

"There is no force more powerful than a woman determined to rise."

— Unknown

Your parents undermine you. Teachers and professors undermine you. Your boss undermines you. Your peers and coworkers undermine you. The media undermines you every day. The government undermines. Big pharma is undermining you. Your church is undermining you. Social media is undermining you. So, you undermine yourself.

Being undermined by others is the most common cause behind leaders losing confidence. Being undermined can leave us embarrassed, frustrated, and even questioning our abilities. It's not a nice place to be. And yet we get undermined all day every day by our education system, the media, and the government.

People and organizations undermining others are trying to manipulate you to follow their agenda through fear. Often, because they lack confidence, they undermine others so they will feel powerful and important.

And it isn't always others who undermine us. We can be guilty of getting lost in our own self-created story, manufacturing future problems that never actually occur; we then end up unable to step back and see the complete picture.

Have you been undermined? Are you living paycheck to paycheck? Are you watching Netflix as your escape from work? Are you addicted to social media? Are you unhappy at home or at work? Are you living someone else's life? Do you live in fear? Does your credit score suck? Are you becoming a disconnected zombie?

I feel your pain. I have been in your shoes many times. I know what it is like to be undermined by my parents, my teachers, and my peers. I know what it means not to have the confidence to live life on my terms, not to follow my dreams or do what I love most. I walked in your shoes for many decades, so I feel your frustration and desire.

In this book, you will learn that being undermined can be your superpower. I'll show you how being a black sheep in your family is an opportunity to be the lion of your family and how you're a born seeker of liberation who can clear the path for the family tree. People who, from a young age, constantly seek to revolutionize beliefs and leave the paths marked by family traditions are criticized, judged, and even rejected, yet they are the ones called to free the tree of repetitive stories that frustrate entire generations. The undermined who do not adapt and who shout rebellion play a basic role within each family system; they repair, detoxify, and create a new and flourishing branch in the family tree. Thanks to these members, our trees renew their roots. Their rebellion becomes the tree's fertile land; their madness is the water that nourishes it; their stubbornness is oxygen; and their passion is the fire that rekindles the courage of their ancestors. Let no one make you doubt; take care of your uniqueness like it is the most precious flower on your tree. You are the dream come true of all your ancestors. This book will give you the tools and insight to your transformation to become an empowered leader. I promise you that after reading this book, you will be inspired, committed to never being undermined again, and act to live your life and your passion.

If you apply the wisdom, knowledge, experience, skills, strategies, and techniques offered in this book to your life, you will become a transformational leader and live a committed and fulfilled life. You will be an example for your family, community, and maybe even humanity.

I wrote this book to share my story, my expertise, my career's ups and downs, my losses and my gains, my fears and my victories, but most importantly, my life experience and my journey to becoming an empowered leader. As my grandmother shared with me, "Life is a lifelong journey of learning and experiences." I don't have all the answers; I'm still learning every single day. But because life is short, I hope this book will give you a shortcut to becoming the person you are destined to be.

I understand why you have not pursued all your dreams, goals, and visions. Life gets in the way and things happen. I know you may be a single parent, working two or three jobs, going to night school, or maybe even living on government care, homeschooling your child, and trying to survive instead of thrive. I want you to know that is okay, and I believe in you. We all have challenges and go through good and bad times. Where you are now is not your destination, just a station on your journey.

I want to be your virtual mentor, your accountability partner. I want to be the shoulder you can lean on during tough times. I want to be your friend, the person and resource you look to for help in overcoming your challenges.

Are you ready to begin? Are you ready to step outside of your box? Are you ready to expand your comfort zone and step into the new person you are becoming? Are you ready to achieve your goals? If so, Great, Let's get started!

Now is your time!

Let's go!

Chapter 1
Undermined No More!

"The greatest pleasure in life is what people say you cannot do."
— Walter Bagehot

Did you ever feel lonely as a child or adult? Did you ever feel abandoned? Have people shut you down or quit you? Do you feel hopeless or held back? Did you get corrected all the time? Have you ever been pushed to do something you didn't want to, like becoming a doctor instead of an entrepreneur? All of these are examples of how people are undermined or let themselves become undermined. They are ways I was undermined myself. Today, my soul lives to its full potential, living out my purpose, passion, and dreams. But that has not always been the case. In fact, it was not for most of my life. Bear with me as I expand on this idea. This is a vulnerable chapter—and the beginning of the journey I'll take you on.

MY STORY

We're all born as confident, happy, abundant, positive spiritual beings who choose to have a human experience. I believe we choose our parents. Looking back, it makes sense to me now, but as a child, I often felt unhappy, not seen for who I was, unheard, and not celebrated for my unique gifts and talents. I'm pretty sure you recognize yourself in this. I grew up in a middle-class neighborhood with a dad who worked for the government and a stay-at-home mom. Their marriage was unhappy, and their many fights daily ruined our joy.

My dad was a strict man with many rules. Very few gaps existed for freedom of expression, being myself, exploring life, or finding my identity.

Connecting the dots backward, and after thousands of hours of personal development, coaching, healing, and growth, I now truly believe parents, teachers, and other influencers direct our lives without our explicit knowledge. That influence can be positive or negative. In my case, my dad, teachers, employers, friends, and even partners significantly undermined me.

My dad corrected me and my two sisters non-stop: walk like a girl, take shorter steps, be more elegant, sit up straight, don't make sounds with your mouth or nose, cross your legs like a girl, don't spread them like a boy, open the door correctly, close the door softly, don't touch the wall, walk up the stairs silently, no running, play quietly, whisper, be quiet, listen, eat with your mouth closed, eat all your food, don't scrape your plate while you eat, don't talk during dinner, speak politely, say thank you, say please, know your place, follow the rules, follow the unspoken rules, close the car door gently, don't touch each other, don't drop food in the car, don't fight, ride your bike on the bike path, ride your bike like a girl. The list goes on and on.

I was a very happy child until about eight. By then, after so many corrections, I started to feel not good enough, not understood, not heard, and not seen. My identical twin sister, Nicole, spoke for me. She had to lead, and many people didn't know the difference between us. We got bullied a lot, so I became quiet and invisible. I didn't feel good enough.

I lost my joy for life. I felt insecure and had low self-esteem. I tried to stay under the radar.

Unfortunately, my teachers did not inspire or provide a positive influence either. I felt like a misfit. I hated school, so I pretended I was sick often just to avoid being shamed, undermined, and harassed.

I didn't have many friends. Being an identical twin made it more challenging to develop my own personality, and I had to fight for my own identity.

> *"Not until we are lost do we begin to understand ourselves."*
> — Henry David Thoreau

I had high hopes, however, when I went to high school. It was a new start with opportunities to be me, be seen, and make new friends. The first two years were good. I had friends, and many people from my school were part of our field hockey club.

I loved playing sports. I loved competition, and I was determined to win. I felt free when I played field hockey, running with my hair in the wind and giving it my all. I had to win for the team. I spent every free moment at the hockey club, training, playing, or just hanging out with my friends.

But under it all, I felt lonely because of all the fighting at home. My parents were very unhappy in their marriage and often emotionally abused one another. (They divorced when I was seventeen.) It was hard on me and my sisters. I thought about suicide a lot. I was afraid of failing and not graduating. I confided in a male teacher at my high school because I could not stand my psychologist. I literally didn't say a word during my sessions with him. I hope I didn't traumatize him.

The teacher manipulated our conversations toward sex, relationships, and "exploration." I was a teen, insecure, unhappy, and afraid to fail—

the perfect victim to emotionally manipulate and sexually abuse. It also happened in the very place that should have been safe—a Catholic school. The teacher touched me sexually for three years until I graduated. Then I never saw him again. Allowing the manipulation and keeping the secret, allowing my soul to be undermined and my body used, and regretting my mental weakness all disgusted me until I realized I couldn't have done anything about it at the time.

I kept this secret until I was in my late thirties. I prayed every night, hoping I was the only victim and no one else had to go through the same experience. Unfortunately, I will never know. I regret not coming forward sooner. At the same time, I questioned for years whether anyone would believe me. Everyone thought he was the nicest and most charismatic man in the school. I speak about it now because I'm involved in stopping sex trafficking and other initiatives to empower young girls and women to speak up when they feel something is not right. Better safe than sorry!

My graduation was supposed to be a happy moment of celebration. Instead, I felt insecure about myself and my future.

I had a chance for a new beginning at the University of Amsterdam. However, many mornings when I waited for the train, I thought about jumping in front of it. My soul had been raped out of me, my heart shattered, and my body not my temple anymore. I fought through it alone, not talking to anyone. I overperformed at the university to distract myself. I worked my job and played field hockey. I didn't like dentistry; I had been talked into it. I didn't know what else to do, so I decided to finish what I had started. Field hockey was my joy and passion. I think that saved my life. When I graduated, I celebrated not quitting and accomplishing more than any teacher ever thought I would. My middle and high school teachers had undermined my intellect and strength to acquire anything beyond a minimal education job. Shame on them.

My first compliment at the university was more than good—it made me feel great! But I still didn't like college; it just helped me finish strong and confident about something besides field hockey.

> *"Once we begin to look for what's right, our lives begin spinning in unimaginably exciting new directions."*
>
> — Pam Grout

At my middle school reunion, I realized how badly the odds had been stacked against me. No one there would believe I was intelligent and talented. I had been ridiculed in front of the class many times. I got bullied and beat up. The reunion was payback time. I was stunned to realize I was the only one there who went to university, graduated, and had a great job. They were surprised. The reunion fueled my drive to become better and better, launching me on a journey of personal development.

Although my life seemed nice on the outside, I was miserable working as a dental hygienist and children's dentist. When I learned the highest suicide rate by profession is in the dental industry—after all, you have to stare all day into dirty, stinky mouths—I started to rethink my career. I asked the Universe, God, and my guides for help and insight into the next step in changing my life.

Boom! There it was!

While riding my bicycle in the Netherlands, I got hit by two motorcycles. They were racing each other while I was crossing the bike path. It was a bloody mess, and I ended up in the hospital for a day of research, conclusions, and treatment. Then they sent me home with a friend.

I had a lot of pain and didn't feel good at all. I couldn't work or play field hockey. Two weeks later, I returned to work, only to faint and be rushed to my sister's house. I went to the hospital several times after that because I didn't feel well, just to be sent home with, "It is all between your ears." A week later when I fainted at home, my girlfriend called an ambulance. (No one knew I had a girlfriend because I had not come out of the closet yet.)

At the hospital, I was rushed to an MRI scan to figure out what was going on. I woke up with eight doctors and nurses around me in the intensive care unit. I discovered doctors were not the best communicators, so it took me a while to figure out what was going on. My body was full of blood clots. My family was called and told I might not survive. My sister Claire worked as a nurse at the hospital. She supported me every day, visited me, and helped me.

In the ICU, I had two near-death experiences and many scary moments. (More on that later.) I spent months in the hospital recovering. I couldn't get out of bed; I couldn't walk; and I had no strength or energy. Everything was mentally taxing. I had to wear a full-body compression suit for eight years. It would be three years before I was able to work full time.

Doing rehab at twenty-three was challenging. My friends were partying, traveling, and having fun. I was at the rehab center, at the gym, seeing a therapist or coach, or at home. My girlfriend Mieke, who later became my first wife, was my rock! She worked the late-night shift at a restaurant. She loved me unconditionally and supported me every step of the way. I'm forever grateful for her.

The doctors told me I couldn't work, play sports, walk, party, fly, or live as I used to. Talk about being undermined.

At that point, I realized I had two choices—be a victim and give in to all the depressing messages, or become a victor and fight myself out of it. I had dreams and plans. I had a life purpose, and now I was on a mission. It was hard, but I knew I wouldn't die from hard work. I watched daily Tony Robbins DVDs in the hospital, hired coaches, took mindfulness courses, read books, and joined workshops and seminars. I went to the gym and hired a personal trainer. I fought a ten-year lawsuit against the motorcyclist who hit me and won. The motorcyclist had to pay all my bills.

I could have blamed all my problems on my parents, teachers, friends, employers, peers, the media, or the motorcyclists, but it wouldn't have made a difference in my life. I believe people handle things the best they can in the moment, and then it is up to us to heal and create a better future for ourselves. It's not an easy task, but it's rewarding. And it leaves us with more inner peace, gratitude, love for others, compassion, and success.

"One of the most fundamental of human fears is that our existence will go unnoticed, and we die with the best still inside of us."

— Esther Wildenberg

LESSONS LEARNED

As a child, I didn't feel worthy. I felt unheard, unseen, unrecognized, and unsafe. I never found my place. I never felt safe to speak my truth. I always asked, "Who am I?" My mom was powerless and unheard; her only power was becoming a mom. My dad didn't know how to show love. My dad didn't feel loved or seen, so he manipulated us by creating an outside picture. I learned our parents just do what they have seen and experienced themselves. However, I believe women have the strength to manipulate energy to fight a man's strength.

I would not have survived the first twenty-five to thirty years of my life without my family in the city of Apeldoorn. My uncle, aunt, and three cousins provided me with a home, a safe place, support, unconditional love, and encouragement. I love them unconditionally. My best memories of the first half of my life are from time spent with them. The memories and the love I feel for them are locked in my heart and mind. It's a great reminder that we only need a *handful* of people who truly love us, believe in us, and support our dreams.

My mom always loved me, but at the time, she was looking for love and confidence in herself. My grandparents loved me but could not support me. Their presence and unconditional love were enough. Find five people who support your dreams and passions and truly see who you are. Sometimes it's not your direct family, but your chosen family, your friends. In my case, it was my aunt, uncle, and three cousins. They're forever in my heart, and I will always love them.

We have to see when someone is making us less confident, less powerful, less likely to succeed, or is making something we created weaker. Often gradually, they're undermining us. It hurts deeply, short term and long term. When we see we are being undermined, it's important to know it's not our fault.

People act in accordance with their own insecurities, beliefs, and patterns. Sometimes it's copied behavior. There's also a difference between undermining and underestimating. Underestimating is assuming something, or someone, is less than it is or they are, that someone is incapable of doing something they can do. Undermining is getting in the way of someone's dreams and plans, redirecting them from their life path and personal journey.

I learned that when you're quiet, you become a better observer and listener. I'm an incredible listener. I ask great questions and truly listen to the answer. I don't think about my story, my example, the wisdom I can share, or my next question. The book *The Body Keeps the Score* by Bessel van der Kolk or *Trauma: Je Bent Gek Als Je Het Niet Hebt* by Christine Pannebakker (for my Dutch readers) are great reads for understanding we all have childhood and adult trauma. Recognize that pain, patterns, stinking thinking, unhealthy behavior, and responses come from trauma, learned behavior, and even from our DNA.

We have to dig in and do the work. I read a book a week, have a personal coach, have a business mentor, and am committed to a lifelong journey of personal growth. As Emile Coue said, "Every day, in every way, I'm getting better and better."

At ninety, in the final stage of her life, my grandmother shared a life lesson I never forgot—it comes up weekly. One day, we had a beautiful heart-to-heart about life and how hard it is. I told her my struggles about learning life lessons, finding yourself, meeting the love of your life (or not), business dynamics, and the past trauma that kept coming up even after a lot of healing. My grandmother said, "I'm ninety years old, and I'm still learning every single day. Life is a journey, and life lessons will never end. Acknowledge it, heal it, believe it, and receive the gift of growing and becoming a better version of yourself."

> *"You have power over your mind, not outside events. Realize this, and you will find strength."*
> — Marcus Aurelius

EXERCISE

Think about the questions below. Then describe how you feel and what action you can take.

1. When have you felt undermined?

_____

_____

_____

2. In which areas do you need healing?

_____
_____
_____
_____

3. Which five people in your life support you unconditionally?

_____
_____
_____
_____
_____

4. Who are you?

_____
_____
_____
_____

5. Who would you be if you knew you couldn't fail?

_____
_____
_____
_____
_____
_____
_____

FIVE TIPS FOR RECOGNIZING WHEN YOU ARE BEING UNDERMINED

1. Anyone squashing your dreams is undermining you.
2. Anyone being racist about your skin color is undermining you.
3. Anyone not showing love and respect for your sexual preference is undermining you.
4. Anyone silencing your voice is undermining you.
5. Anyone diminishing your creativity is undermining you.

SUMMARY

Most often, the people undermining you are doing it unconsciously. Many are insecure or have low self-esteem. They are most likely mimicking learned behavior from their parents and grandparents. They're afraid of the light and brightness, so fear for you unnecessarily. They look up to you in a certain way. They don't understand the path you're on. They don't believe in themselves, so they cannot support you. They may be jealous of your determination. They don't understand your personal growth and feel left behind.

The best way to connect to your spiritual nature and stop being undermined is to follow your joy. I wanted to be the first—the first to break the mold and stop the cycle. I dared to believe in breaking generational patterns. You can too. And you can affect generations to come! You can create something that changes the world, but it's worth it just to change yourself and your family. Maybe you are the first one to go to college or live beyond poverty. Maybe you are the first to dream big. Maybe you are the first to become a humanitarian, to travel the world, to have more than a million dollars in your bank account, or to love boldly and live genuinely happy from your soul.

Here's to all the "crazy" ones. The ones who think differently, act uniquely, and believe in the impossible. Here's to never quitting on your wildly optimistic dreams and visions. I love the courage and unpopularity of dreamers.

Never shrink or hide. Get up and let your visions and passions be known. You could be a generational leader in your family, changing the future of your lineage. It all starts with healing your heart, being your highest self, and breaking the glass ceiling. Believe in yourself, not others—just in you. You're on your own unique journey. No one can walk your path, no one can save you, and no one can do the work for you. It's up to you.

> *"Accept responsibility for your life. Know that it is you who will get you where you want to go, no one else."*
>
> — Les Brown

CALL TO ACTION

I challenge you never to play small again. Set boundaries to keep others from undermining you. Do not let others' opinions dim your light. Step into your power and believe in your divine right to be you. I encourage you to never be undermined again. And most importantly, don't undermine yourself!

"You yourself, as much as anybody in the entire universe, deserve your love and affection."

— Sharon Salzberg

Chapter 2

Unleashing the Tiger

"Your unique creative talents and abilities are flowing through you and are being expressed in deeply satisfying ways. Your creativity is always in demand."

— Louise Hay

What needs to happen to live your dream life? Have you ever felt like your wings were clipped? Do you feel you live in a cage? Are you trapped inside your own mind? Do you know you have more inside of you? Are you playing small because of others?

MY STORY

The first twenty-three years of my life, I lived as expected of me, being a great student, playing sports, dating boys, and listening to my parents, teachers, and friends. And I was deeply unhappy with my life. I felt I couldn't be me. I felt locked within my own mind and body.

Over the past twenty-seven years, I've unleashed the tiger inside in several ways. I knew I had the power to live the life I wanted. Over the years, the baby tiger became a big tiger, so my power got stronger. I had hopes and dreams, and the only way to pursue them was to break free of the box, the cage I grew up in, and the cage I created many times over the years for myself.

I knew I had to become better in so many areas—my relationships, my mindset, my beliefs, my finances, and in healing my heart.

After my accident at twenty-three, I was motivated to live bigger and better. I was hungry for my new life. I journaled a lot about my dreams and the things I wanted to accomplish. I set five- and ten-year goals. After my near-death experiences, my vision and mission became clear, and I knew I was not ready yet. I didn't share my vision and dreams until I was thirty-three. I spent ten years developing myself into a great coach, consultant, retreat host, and mastermind facilitator.

But I often talked myself out of my dreams. I ridiculed myself for thinking anyone wanted my experience and wisdom. Still, I kept opening the cage door little by little. I also realized when you don't share your passion, no one can support you. I started to share my coaching and consulting ideas with my friend Jasper. He supported me and helped me open my first business, build my website, craft my messaging and branding, and boost my confidence.

"You are the one you've been looking for."

— Danny Morel

I took the big leap. I swung the cage door wide open. I quit my six-figure job to start my own business.

But I didn't have a lot of support. My family thought I was taking too big of a risk and didn't have the expertise to make a living as an entrepreneur. I was confident enough to know that was their limiting belief—it had nothing to do with me. My dad worked for the government for thirty-five years, my mom worked at the hospital, and everyone in my family had nine-to-five jobs, except my cousin who was also a budding entrepreneur. All my friends had regular jobs, except Jasper, who supported me and introduced me to my first consulting client.

As my business grew, I acquired clients mostly among the Fortune 500. I started to collaborate with other consulting firms and developed long-term relationships with my network in the Netherlands.

At the same time, I promoted my first retreat in France. I had to act on my intuition, follow my compass, and have faith in the idea that the right people always show up. I was honored to have six people show up at that first retreat, held in a farmhouse. It was a magical experience. They loved it so much that three of them came again a few months later.

Soon, I was off to the races, hosting three or four retreats a year. I held retreats in Spain, Bali, Sri Lanka, Thailand, Mexico, Dominican Republic, Ibiza, and many more countries. Nothing is more fulfilling than seeing people transform in one week, step into their power, and embrace their talents.

I worked with other amazing coaches to expand, helping mostly women really step into their life purpose and own it. When you heal your heart, you find clarity; then you can listen to your soul and your heart's desires. Magic happens when you let go of what doesn't serve you and start stepping into the light of your future.

> *"You never know how strong you are until being strong is your only choice."*
>
> — Bob Marley

In October 2013, I met my second wife, Cheri, at a conference in Amsterdam. She was one of the keynote speakers, and I bought her BANK program, which incorporates personality identification with real-world sales best practices to accelcrate my consulting and retreat business. I used and sold the BANK system in Europe. In February of 2014, Cheri and I traveled through Europe together and fell in love.

Eight months later, I moved to the United States to live with her. I left behind thirty-nine years in the Netherlands, my business, clients, community, network, home, and stuff. I had worked hard to keep my family and friends close. Moving was not an easy decision; it changed my life forever. More about that later.

I was happy, but at the same time, I felt like I was back in my cage. Everything I had built in the Netherlands was gone. I had to start from scratch, and English was not my native language. I worked in Cheri's company, but after a year, I told Cheri I really wanted to host retreats again. I created the Personal Banker program for our company, Codebreaker Technologies. I hosted two retreats a year for our certified trainers, and I was coaching again, living part of my talents. The cage was open, and I could shine as a retreat host, coach, and business expert. The program evolved over the years, and we facilitated it for eight years until the pandemic happened. As we all know, 2020 was an interesting year. I think we all felt locked in cages in our own way.

With so much experience, I was ready to break the cage and fly high. No more cage for me. In addition to being the cofounder and president of Codebreaker Technologies, I started to speak on stages about world class leadership, spiritual intelligence in business, and the power of healing your heart, not just your mind. I helped several consulting clients grow their businesses, strengthen their leadership teams, and expand their vision.

In 2024, we launched our new mastermind program, ICONIC X. This concept helps entrepreneurs and business owners live an ICONIC life by mastering the eight forms of wealth and the eight intelligences to help people feel fulfilled in all aspects of life, not just money or relationships.

As I write this book, I am living my life outside the cage. I do what I love, helping others by speaking, writing, consulting, coaching, and facilitating retreats with people from around the world. No more cage—the world is my stage.

> *"There is a tiger inside all of us just waiting to be unleashed."*
> — Esther Wildenberg

LESSONS LEARNED

Being in a cage is like being in prison. Don't allow others to put you there, and don't put yourself there.

We often allow others to put us there. But look for the lesson in every situation. I allowed some to clip my wings and put me in a cage. I didn't stop them. Most do more for others than for themselves. We have to find balance between doing for ourselves and serving others.

When you focus on daily progress and know you're a lifelong learner, you'll grow to recognize when someone is trying to cast their shadow over you. Overcoming is all about taking the time to appreciate your experiences and never stop learning. Each moment offers a lesson to help you fully step into your potential so you can leave the cage behind for good.

Embracing the power of possibility is the beginning of being able to successfully unleash your full potential. You can achieve great things by recognizing your potential, confronting your limiting beliefs, and cultivating a growth mindset. Don't let anything stand in the way of achieving excellence, whatever that looks like for you.

It is also critical to seek out the skills, mindset, and characteristics you must develop to achieve your goals and unleash your potential. At some point while attempting to achieve audacious goals that stretch and challenge you, you must become a completely different person. And when you feel that shift, all cages disappear from your life.

We are the people we regularly associate with. It is crucial to be deliberate about who gets your time and energy and to ensure the people you associate with help you become a better version of yourself rather than diminishing your talent or life purpose. Unfortunately, I have far too many examples of people who failed to unleash their potential because of the people they were associated with, including myself. Being intentional about who you let in and focusing on those who will help you become the best version of yourself is essential for unleashing your potential. You have no room for a prison or cage in your life anymore. Your time is now.

> *"Prison is itself a tremendous education in the need for patience and perseverance. It is, above all, a test of one's commitment...."*
>
> — Nelson Mandela

You have the power to create your destiny by mastering your thoughts, emotions, and behavior. When you set ambitious, inspiring goals, you get excited about pursuing them; that creates motivation and momentum, even in the face of challenges. It takes courage. Some try too hard to avoid future disappointment and often stop creating clearly defined, actionable goals to get what they want in their lives physically, spiritually, mentally, emotionally, and financially—instead, their goals are merely to get by, pay bills, and survive. They don't realize their past failures may not be due to personal shortcomings. Knowing and living by your values brings deep fulfillment, inner peace, certainty, and joy. If you're unclear about your values, or if you have conflicting values, it can cause enduring unhappiness and frustration. Get clear on your values, your life purpose, your passion, your goals and legacy. With clarity, you will be unstoppable.

Moving forward, you'll practice mastering your relationships—specifically, your romantic or other significant relationships—because relationships are not only essential to your well-being, but also powerful forces influencing your beliefs, values, and fears. You can do anything you decide to do. You can act to change and control your life, and the procedure, the process is its own reward. You'll enjoy the successful and empowered life you're creating even more if you have someone to share it with.

Change yourself, then change the world.

Countless problems and tragedies constantly happen across the globe. Joint decisions, made collectively by the world's population, determine whether we surrender to or overcome these problems. It's up to every person to make individual choices that contribute to joint decisions and solutions—including you. You know you have the power to make individual decisions. Now participate in joint decisions to change communities, societies, nations, and the world. When you're unleashed, there's no going back. When the tiger is free, she thrives; she's fearless, courageous, and unstoppable in reaching her dreams.

> *"I feel like a tiger right now. There's nothing impossible if you get up and work for it."*
>
> — Michael Flatley

EXERCISE

Looking at the questions below, describe what you think, how you feel, and what action you could take.

1. When did you feel trapped in a cage?

_____
_____
_____
_____

2. Do you remember when you locked up the tiger inside you?

_____
_____
_____
_____

3. Who in your life caged you?

_____
_____
_____
_____
_____

4. What would you be doing without the cage?

_____
_____
_____
_____
_____

5. Who would you be if the tiger inside was unleashed?

_____
_____
_____
_____
_____
_____
_____

FIVE TIPS FOR KEEPING THE TIGER UNLEASHED

1. Anyone who tries to put you in a cage should be removed from your inner circle.
2. Anyone who does not like your strength, power, and truth is not your audience.
3. Anyone who does not support you in living in your own spotlight is not a real friend.
4. Anyone in your life should know you don't like to be caged; you need space.
5. Anyone who tries to stop you will meet the tiger inside.

SUMMARY

The tiger is a magnificent animal with its splendid carriage and sinuous grace. Adult tigers have no natural enemies. Although largely protected from human hunting, pressure from civilization and development has kept the tiger population on the verge of extinction. Don't let the tiger inside you go extinct!

Tigers are handsome and powerful, with innate self-confidence and elegance. Female tigers have a sense of immediacy and an aura of electricity surrounding them; when they walk into a room, it feels like something is about to happen. Once a tiger has found its groove, it will focus on its goal with a brightly burning intensity. Male tigers, when out of their element, are sometimes mistaken for beefcake, but when you see them in their offices wearing their power suits, you'll soon realize you're dealing with incisive, authoritative people. In social situations, the tiger is an excellent host—there is no such thing as a casual party in its home. Guests can always expect a memorable occasion with extravagant food and drink, and yet, a tiger has a distinct coldness. Having sacrificed comfort for style, the tiger outfits its house with austere and modern furniture, and comfortably worn easy chairs are replaced every few years.

Tigers are solitary creatures who hate to lie around doing nothing. In this regard they have more in common with wild cats and leopards, who are always on the move, and because of this antisocial aspect, it can be difficult to discern a tiger's true motives: They are considered unpredictable and enigmatic. They have a strong aversion to routine in daily life, and their spontaneity and energy infect others graced with their presence. Tigers dislike small talk in the workplace and expect professionalism from coworkers, demanding the highest standards in their business dealings. With their killer instincts, tigers make excellent trial lawyers and do not hesitate to use aggression to their advantage. Acutely aware of their ability to intimidate, tigers' single-mindedness enhances their reputation as a force to be reckoned with.

Because of their preference for solitude, however, tigers are not natural leaders. While perfectly capable of assuming the role of CEO, they prefer the challenges inherent in self-employment. Tiger businesses are invariably successful and cover a wide range of industries, from engineering to retailing, and from top salespeople to spiritual gurus. Their instinct and intuition are not to be argued with—when they know, they know. When you truly step into the tiger you are, the world is your playground. You will change lives, influence humanity, and be successful in every area of your life. All you need to do is live free. It's time to live your life like a tiger.

"A tiger never loses sleep over the opinion of sheep."
— Ziad K. Abdelnour

CALL TO ACTION

Get out of your cage and explore your freedom. Set boundaries to keep others from putting you in a cage. Embrace the beautiful soul you are and own your space. Recognize when you want to hide in your invisible cage. Never be trapped again. Stretch your muscles and claim your life.

Chapter 3

Manifesting Abundance

"When you are grateful, fear disappears, and abundance appears."

— Tony Robbins

Have you ever felt fear? Do you sometimes think others are lucky? Did you ever think of something and suddenly it showed up? Did you know when it comes to abundance, gratitude is everything? Do you believe you will be more successful or financially free than your parents? Let me share with you how I came to create abundance in my own life.

MY STORY

The link between gratitude and success took me a long time to understand. I have always been curious about quantum time and exploring the unknown and invisible. This might sound woo woo to you, and that's okay. Follow me, and you'll see you're living it every day through your thoughts, wishes, dreams, communication, journal, and social media posts.

The energy of gratitude is the energy of already having; it says what you want is already here.

The Universe sends things to you that match *what you are already*—so whatever you see in your reality is a mirror of your energy.

When you have gratitude for something you don't yet see in your physical reality, it will come to you…because you've chosen to tell the Universe it's already yours!

Have you ever noticed that if you want to create the life of your dreams, you must be willing to do things differently than everyone else?

People are so programmed with limiting beliefs and old paradigms that they don't even realize how much it's keeping them small. Those people include my own family. They believe religion and the church is the only way to happiness and success. Now, I'm going to rattle some feathers. As a ten-year-young girl, I remember challenging my grandmother about God and the Bible. I asked her uncomfortable questions like: "Who says God is a man? Maybe it's a woman, maybe there is no God. Who wrote the Bible?" I then told my grandmother I didn't want to pray by a script or book, I didn't want to go to church, and there was no need to kneel to connect with the Divine.

The conversation didn't end as I had hoped. I was innocent, and I meant every word I said. My grandmother told me to just follow her and respect her by listening to what she thought was best. Her response is how we pass on false or unfounded beliefs and stinking thinking and manipulate the next generation. What if we let every child develop their own faith, their own connection to Source, their own curious thinking, and let them live their own unique path in this lifetime?

God is one; it's the energy of love. It's not some dude who died for us. It's the field of Infinite Potentiality, Source, Divine. God, the Higher Source, never judges and just wants joy and love. God as a concept has become warped and misused. It's a closed concept that's the opposite of truth. Religion creates separation, judgment, fear, low vibration, war, and small thinking. It's manipulative, brainwashing minds and beliefs and dictating what to do and what not to do. It tells us how to think and separates us from others, including our own family.

When you operate at low vibrating levels, you're an easy target for manipulation. God is available to you without spending a penny. Some churches operate at a low vibration, using shame, guilt, fear, and anger to control people. I have news for you. Hell does not exist. The devil was invented to keep you in line. Heaven sees no rank, no separation. Stop thinking the church is going to save you.

Surrender and experience God as it is, love!

The church is just a community like any other community where we sell our ideas, products, beliefs, and service. It's just whichever idea you believe is best for you. But one is no better than another. You are your own salvation.

God has no gender—why would an infinite, eternal force need a gender? God is not human. God is the energy of love. God is one. You and God are one. You're a spiritual being having a human experience. And when we return to the Divine Source, we all go to the same place, called love.

I learned over time when you live in the higher vibration realm, you can manifest anything positive. When you operate at lower vibration levels, you attract more negativity into your life. We all have the power to manifest what we want—and what we don't want if we don't watch our thoughts and words carefully.

> *"Most brainpower is devoted to old beliefs, scarcity, problems, and what ifs. That is why your mindset sucks. Change your thinking into feeling gratitude and everything will change."*
>
> — Esther Wildenberg

LESSONS LEARNED

The energy of gratitude is the energy of already having; it's already here right now.

You have unlimited potential when you're willing to think differently from everyone else. You can build a business that makes money all day, every day, even when you're traveling, even in your sleep.... But you will need to break free of the belief a paycheck every two weeks is the only way to feel "secure." It's not! Be willing to be true to yourself and not follow the crowd. You'll be amazed by how much abundance you can attract when you're truly being you.

One energy that goes with abundance is love.

Love is at the center of everything I do, and I truly believe that's why I've been able to build a multimillion-dollar tech company, speaker business, retreat-mastermind business, and consulting business.

I love myself. I love my purpose and passion to help others succeed.

I love my business. I love my clients. I love my business partners. I love my family and friends. And I love who I have become and the life I've created for myself because of it. At the end of the day, all the abundance we create is all about love. We often think we'll be rich when we get money, feel successful when we reach a certain goal, be happy when we find the love of our life, but it doesn't work like that.

> *"If beating ourselves up worked, we'd all be rich, skinny, and happy by now."*
>
> — Cheryl Richardson

EXERCISE

1. Write your *new* money story.

_____
_____
_____
_____
_____
_____
_____
_____

2. What's your financial dream?

_____
_____
_____
_____
_____
_____
_____

3. What's your ideal relationship?

_____
_____
_____
_____
_____
_____
_____
_____

4. What does perfect health look like for you?

_____
_____
_____
_____
_____
_____
_____
_____
_____

5. What's your dream for your future?

_____
_____
_____
_____
_____
_____
_____
_____
_____
_____
_____

FIVE TIPS FOR MANIFESTING ANYTHING YOU WANT

1. Think about what you really want. Be specific. Don't let anyone stop you.
2. Describe in detail what you want in your journal. Keep it private.
3. Feel the emotions; feel how you will feel when it shows up. Write it in your journal.

4. Speak it out loud into the universe with intention and belief.
5. Be ready to receive it and welcome the right people when they show up.

SUMMARY

Stop surviving and start living—thrive. The key to manifesting anything you want is understanding you are a limitless being. When you forgive yourself and others, the portal will open. Forgive yourself, your stinking thinking, the pain you caused others, and the decisions you made. Forgive your parents, your siblings, your family, the person who abused you, your friends, your teachers and professors, your partners, your business relationships, and anyone who hurt you in the past. Say, "I'm sorry. Please forgive me. Thank you. I love you." You can do this in your mind and feel it in your heart. You can do it in person. And you can even do it with ones who've moved on to the other side. We're all energy; we're all one; we're all connected. Let go of the old story and create a new one.

> *"The universe is limitless, abundant, and strangely accommodating."*
>
> — Pam Grout

Whatever you imagine, you can have. Think it. Write it. Feel it. Speak it. Receive it. And repeat it. The following is a powerful script that really works:

> In the next forty-eight hours, I request [blank]. I align my attention. Thank you. I request that in the next six months I will [blank]. I align my attention to it. Thank you.

Think about it—the goals you want to achieve are mostly about the "feeling" you want to experience. When you're in the energy of having *more than enough*—the energy of being confident and in control—everything else will fall into place. That is how it works. It's not doing all the things, feeling stressed out, and then hoping it'll work out. It's being in the energy of it working out, that's when it shows up in your physical reality. You must decide now. It's a choice only you can make. Only you can act on what you believe.

> "Now you decide you're successful. You decide you live in abundance.
>
> "You decide you can change the world. You decide you're in a love relationship. You decide you're speaking on stage for 5,000 people.
>
> "You decide everything you want is already yours. You decide you're healthy. You decide you're living in your dream home. You decide you're on the vacation of your dreams. You decide now.
>
> "Any pain coming to you is to help you ascend, grow, forgive, let go, surrender to love, and to have it all."
>
> — Esther Wildenberg

CALL TO ACTION

I encourage and give you permission to start manifesting small things first. Be grateful for each blessing. Dream bigger than ever before. Step into your dream by taking massive action. I inspire you to give more to others. Giving makes you happy.

"See yourself living in abundance and you will attract it."
— Bob Proctor

Chapter 4

Embracing Your Voice

"The human voice is the most beautiful instrument of all, but it is the most difficult to play."

— Richard Strauss

Have you silenced yourself? Are you struggling to find your voice or just be heard? Have you ever wondered "What if people laugh at me?" Have other people silenced you? Do people interrupt you all the time? Are you afraid of your own power and light? Are you afraid of being too much? Do you think you're not good enough? Are you afraid of speaking your truth?

MY STORY

For most of my childhood, I didn't speak. I didn't use my voice, much less embrace its power. I was silenced by my dad and my twin sister Nicole. They didn't do it to hurt me. They were just trying to overcome their own struggles with having a voice. And then I silenced myself. I thought I was supposed to be quiet and not disturb conversations or stand up for myself in a fight.

I was a very quiet child with low self-esteem. I lacked confidence and really didn't want the spotlight on me. I didn't like to talk at big family gatherings where everyone was watching me. I was happy to open my birthday gift and say thank you, but that was probably it. Nicole spoke most of the time for both of us anyway. When someone asked, "How are you?" she would answer, "We are doing great!" In school, the teachers made fun of me when I didn't know the answer. I cried my eyes out when I had to speak in front of the class. I hated doing presentations. When we had group experiments, I always voted for someone else to present.

That all changed in my twenties. My rehab was hard, and at the same time, it was the best thing that ever happened to me. I did so much healing, coaching, stepping into my power, finding my voice, and sharing my truth, my passion, my why, that my emotions became much easier to regulate. My personal development journey helped me to be confident, and I knew I was smart, good looking, strong, funny, sweet, loyal, and generous. I started sharing my ideas, thoughts, and solutions in business meetings and took more and more initiative. People started to listen. Several companies embraced my leadership, and it put me on the path to success.

In my thirties, I started to speak more and more in my corporate job. I had to lead big C-suite meetings and train my sales teams. My clients were mostly Fortune 500 companies, so I had to be strong in conversations, push back, negotiate, and serve at the highest level with kindness and deliver on my promises. I started to embrace the power of my voice. My smile became my superpower. The words started to come more and more easily. Talking became fun. Speaking about my ideas and truths became more natural. My confidence was high, and I started to share jokes and funny stories to make people laugh. I was often asked to speak at funerals. I'm not saying I was not nervous. My legs were shaking because I still had the negative little voice in my head. I just didn't listen to it.

> *"The voice is a muscle, and it deserves as much attention and care as any other part of the body."*
> — Adele

When I turned forty, I started speaking on stages from small rooms with a hundred people to big conventions centers with thousands. I had no professional speaker training. I watched many speakers over the years—my wife Cheri is one of the best speakers I have ever heard. She was a great mentor by just putting me out there on her stages. Prepared or not, ready or not, she just called me on stage. I never knew when she would do it.

I'm still too shy to sing out loud or take the lead singing a song. Sometimes I don't feel like speaking. I must be moved, inspired, or hurt to share my message. The power is doing it in a calm but intentional way. Knowing what you want the outcome to be always helps you speak or be quiet. Sometimes more power is found in silence than trying to make your point. As they say, "You can either be right, or you can be kind."

> *"Your voice is your identity. It reveals everything about who you are, how you feel, and what you stand for. It reveals your power."*
> — Esther Wildenberg

LESSONS LEARNED

When you lose your voice, you feel unheard. Then you have the distinct impression that it doesn't matter how often or how loud you say something because no one is listening. Few things are more demoralizing than realizing no one is listening to you. Often, it's like you're having one conversation, and they are having another. You get used to the fact that no one is listening, and everyone else gets used to you not speaking up.

We often operate out of fear rather than on purpose. We have thoughts. Our mind takes us into rabbit holes filled with "What if?" or "I wish." "What if people laugh at me?" or "I wish I had the courage to speak up." These are popular but overrated thoughts. How many times have they come true? How did that serve you? Most people spend years in the same job, relationship, cage, and have worked hard to become a "team player," learning the language of just going with the flow, fitting in, being normal, and not rocking the boat.

When you spend years carefully crafting your course under the radar and how you will fit into the box offered as your path to success, you just might wake up one day wondering who the heck you really are. Trust me, I've been there. A life-altering event—an accident at twenty-three—and becoming a mom at forty-six became catalysts for my personal and professional evolution. I used my fear as a driving force, propelling me toward a path of resilience and grit.

I think many of us grew up in a household, culture, church, community, or family where we were taught to keep silent, not share our dirty laundry, and not be too much. We were made to feel we were not enough, dumb, our voice was too loud, or we were too weird. We learned we were not smart enough to speak, etc. We give our power away so often, caving to others' opinions. Sadly, that's how we undermine our voice when we're young. We don't know any better. As adults, we have the choice to live differently. We don't have to do what others tell us to do rather than sharing our own opinion. We can quit thinking, *If I do like everyone else, I will have the same success they have. The world is telling me what to do, so I'm going to follow what they say instead of listening to my gut.*

When I became an entrepreneur, I had to figure out what worked for me—what I wanted to do, stand for, embody, and represent. That isn't uncommon for entrepreneurs. I started to use my gut more, my common sense, and did my own research. I surrounded myself with people smarter than I am, people who lived the life I wanted to live, the people with the tools, training, and technology to lift me to the next level. My story stands as a testament to the transformative power of our voice and its ability to influence our personal and professional lives.

Your voice—your opinions, ideas, wisdom—is your bridge to others. No matter how invisible you feel, someone is watching you. Someone admires you. Someone would value connecting with you and embracing your thoughts and opinions. It might be that shy coworker, your son, or your younger sister who's in the middle of a big life decision. Your voice matters.

Others only receive what you put out there. You could be sharing someone else's message or beliefs, or the beliefs you currently hold about yourself that you don't want them to know. A curated public image only holds up for so long. You can't just present a single side of yourself to the world—you aren't one-dimensional. It's not that they need to see more, but you need them to see more. You need to be seen too.

> *"Your beliefs also influence the intonation and inflection in your voice, which also influences how other people receive your voice."*
>
> — Unknown

The good news is you're never too far gone or too old. But building your voice is hard work. It might even look like demolition and reconstruction work. I found that process to be integral to rediscovering my voice—and the work is still ongoing.

I would be lying if I didn't tell you that at times I wanted to quit. I questioned everything. I questioned if I was doing what I was supposed to be doing. Was I supposed to continue on this path? Should I pivot? Should I stop altogether? Should I do something else? Should I just be a mom for a while and enjoy this time with my son Kai?

If you don't already know, when you suppress who you are, what you think, believe, and stand for, you will not be happy. More than being happy, I want to feel like what I do matters. Understanding, claiming, and living within the power of my voice gives me the satisfaction of knowing I'm on the road to "fulfilling my potential." I want to know that when I get up each morning, the work I do matters, even if it only matters to me.

> *"When you're on your deathbed, what do you want to be remembered for? And if it's not what you're doing right now, maybe it is time to contemplate what it would look like to make a change. Your legacy happens when you're alive, not when you're dead. You will never regret the things you have done, but you will always regret the things you didn't do."*
>
> – Esther Wildenberg

Realizing you are unique, you are different, can feel isolating at first. But when you realize your uniqueness is the gift you have to offer the world, it will set you free. You will be free to be exactly who you were created to be, to do the things you were created to do. You are the gift. When you take full ownership of your voice, you can step into the fullest expression of who you're meant to be because your voice is like a fingerprint. We each have limiting assumptions, beliefs, and conditioning, but we must overcome them. Your voice matters: It holds immense transformative power—for you and for others. And finally, stop taking advice from people more messed up than you. Don't use their words as your truth.

> *"The message behind the words is the voice of heart."*
>
> — Rumi

EXERCISE

1. Take a good hard look in the mirror and ask yourself the real reason you're afraid to share your opinion and speak your truth?
   _____
   _____
   _____

2. What is unique to your voice?
   _____
   _____
   _____

3. What message do you have inside that the world deserves to hear?
   _____
   _____
   _____
   _____

4. What topics do you avoid and why?
   _____
   _____
   _____

5. Write your deathbed, tombstone message.
   _____
   _____
   _____
   _____
   _____
   _____
   _____

FIVE TIPS FOR EMBRACING THE POWER OF YOUR VOICE

1. Own your uniqueness, your unique voice.

2. Write your personal story and start sharing it with people.

3. Know that an opinion is just an opinion, nothing more, nothing less.

4. Speak out loud. Your audience will show up.

5. Be ready to be surprised by how many people love your voice.

SUMMARY

The first step to reclaiming your voice is understanding the underlying fears and beliefs that led you to silence yourself. Reflect on experiences or trauma that might have shaped your reluctance to express your true thoughts. Don't live in fear of upsetting others or let the desire to be perceived as nice dictate your choices. Don't allow self-imposed restrictions to stifle your voice, preventing you from passionately sharing your belief in living a life of your own design. In a world where fitting in is often celebrated and standing out can be met with skepticism, you find yourself unconsciously trading authenticity for conformity. You may be afraid that speaking your truth and encouraging others to live boldly would alienate the people around you. The desire to be liked can be overpowering, overshadowing your genuine desire to help others create fulfilling lives.

Realize silencing yourself is not only detrimental to your growth but also to the people you could potentially influence positively. By choosing to speak up, you could inspire change, instigate self-discovery, and motivate others to embrace their passions. It is time to break free from the cage and unleash the power of your voice.

EMBRACING YOUR VOICE

"It took me quite a long time to develop a voice, and now that I have it, I am not going to be silent."

— Madeleine Albright

Breaking free from the fear of criticism is easier when you have a support system that encourages and uplifts you. Seek out like-minded individuals who value authenticity and have already embraced their own voices. Engage in conversations with people who genuinely appreciate your passion and perspective, and don't be afraid to share your thoughts openly with them. Surround yourself with supportive, confident, successful, and happy people.

Overcoming the fear of expressing your voice doesn't have to involve a grand, life-altering proclamation. Begin by speaking up in situations where you feel comfortable and confident.

I challenged myself to start writing publicly, on social media, on stage, in magazines, on podcasts, and in other spaces where I could gradually express my beliefs and experiences. The more the positive responses poured in, the more I felt emboldened to embrace my voice fully. The more I spoke out, the more my fear of criticism diminished. The key is to start small and speak out loud.

"The right people will always hear you. You can never say the wrong thing to the right people. The wrong people won't hear you, and that's a blessing."

— Esther Wildenberg

Embracing my true voice and overcoming my fear of expressing my voice was a transformative journey. It wasn't always easy, and I still have moments of doubt, but the joy of empowering others far outweighs any criticism I may receive. Today, I encourage you to take those first steps toward embracing your authentic self so you, too, can make a positive difference in the world around you. Remember, your voice matters, and you have the power to create a life of purpose and fulfillment.

CALL TO ACTION

I encourage you to start speaking your truth. Share your story boldly with people.

Love the beauty of your own voice. Stop listening to people and sources that don't even know you. Take life less seriously, have more fun, and be funny.

"Our lives begin to end the day we become silent about the things that matter."

— Martin Luther King, Jr.

Chapter 5

Climbing the Mountain

"Mountaintops inspire leaders, but valleys mature them."

— Winston Churchill

Have you ever climbed a mountain? What lesson did you learn? Do you feel you're climbing Mount Everest in your day-to-day life and/or business? Are you sitting in a mountain meadow by yourself? Are you standing at the bottom of a mountain with no idea how to get to the top? Let me share a story of how I climbed a mountain—literally!

MY STORY

In my thirties, I went to Sri Lanka for three weeks. Sri Lanka is all about nature and hiking the sacred summit of Adam's Peak because it offers some of the best natural sights, including a one-of-a-kind sunrise you can catch from the top. So, I climbed it! We started our climb late at night. It was very dark, and all we had were our headlamps. It was foggy, misty, humid, and slippery, and breathing was challenging because of the elevation. The hike was six kilometers one way, but it took us around six hours of non-stop climbing to reach the top. Adam's Peak is a pilgrimage for Buddhists. I love being in spiritual environments that bring us deeper into our soul connection, divine purpose, and passions. It was quiet, except for some birds, unknown sounds in the dark of night, and people huffing and puffing.

> *"Climbing is an artistic, creative thing; it's about being spontaneous, traveling, seeing the world, hanging out. It's a balance of setting goals while enjoying the process, being ambitious without being too competitive."*
>
> — Unknown

The climb was hard physically and emotionally. As we climbed, I thought, *Just one step at a time and you will reach the top. Don't stop; just keep going. Stay in the flow; keep your momentum. Don't focus on the pain. Think about the gain, the view, the accomplishment, the sunrise, and the feeling of making it to the top!* I'm very competitive, more with myself than with others. I like to finish what I start. I like to challenge myself. My legs were not too happy about my adventure, but I didn't give it much thought at first.

> *"Somewhere between the bottom of the climb and the summit is the answer to the mystery why we climb."*
>
> — Greg Child

I was wearing full-leg compression socks in the heat and humidity. At that time, I was still taking blood thinners. After climbing for six hours, we reached the top. The view was stunning—the sunrise, the energy, the quiet, and the solitude of sitting on top of the mountain overlooking the beauty of God's creation. The sun was rising, and daylight came over us. I had a beautiful meditative experience.

While I was writing in my journal, I saw blood all over my hiking pants and wondered what had happened. I looked at my legs, pants, socks, hiking shoes—they were all drenched in blood. When I called the guide over, his eyes got big. He told me in broken English I had to take off everything. At that moment, my eyes got really big, not because I had to undress in front of strangers, but because I had tons of leeches stuck to my legs, enjoying my thin, easy-flowing blood. As painful as it sounds, I didn't feel anything. The guide pulled them off, one at a time. It was a fascinating experience.

Like many things, it wasn't as bad as it looked at first. After an hour break on top of the mountain, we started our climb down the mountain. It was much harder than climbing up. My legs were shaking while trying to keep my balance. My legs hurt, and it took so much focus to keep my balance. The climb down took as long as the climb up. It was hard, so I decided to enjoy the scenery, the beauty, the mountains, the rice fields, and the tea plantations. I encouraged the others to keep going.

When we got back to the little village, I was exhausted. I couldn't feel my legs anymore, and I just wanted a hot bath, a massage, and to lay down. I got none of that; we had to get back to the minivan to drive to our hotel two hours away. The drive felt like days. It was uncomfortable. I tried to focus on my experience and the memory I had created, which would last a lifetime—that's what adventure and traveling does.

Historically, mountains have been widely used as metaphors for spiritual awakenings, obstacles humans must face, and the ups and downs of life. The mountain you create in your mind is the obstacle between you and the life you want to live. The mountain shows you all the imperfections, experiences, insecurities, and hardships you've faced so far. They have come together and built up over time to form your personal challenge, the one you must overcome to grow. Our purpose is to grow and reach our true inner potential. Whether we like it or not, we all mature every day. However, the way we react to this process will decide the success of our endeavors. Your old self cannot sustain your new, ever-changing life. To tap into your highest potential, you must reinvent yourself. To do so, you'll have to release trauma and your old mindset and move forward with an improved frame of mind and a pure spirit.

This cycle will repeat itself many times over the course of your lifetime.

I have climbed many metaphorical mountains: health, sports, business, career, travel, relationships, and my spiritual journey. I know there will be many more because they are part of life. It's in my Capricorn DNA to take on hard things, challenges, and opportunities. I like to be the best, reach the top, and live my best life. However, my success didn't come overnight, and I've often wanted to quit climbing.

One big mountain was restoring my health after my accident. Getting back in shape; regaining energy, power, and health; and resuming activities was a huge mountain to climb. I wanted to quit many times and let myself slide back to zero. But I just kept taking one day at a time, one step after the other, not giving up until I was back at the top, back at my powerful, healthy, energetic self.

In my career, I always aimed for the higher mountain, the next position up, the next level of growth and leadership. The corporate world can be tough. I worked most of my career with men only. Working with men made me stronger, less emotionally triggered, and more masculine. It also made me less serious—men make many dumb jokes, mostly sex related. All you can really do is laugh and joke back. When you meet them at their level, you're one of them. And when they weren't watching, I was climbing to the mountaintop. I had positions men dreamed off, mostly older men. I crushed some dreams, but not on purpose. I was just committed to climbing my mountain. When you're focused on your goal, you must stay focused and not get distracted by others or unimportant stuff.

Emotions up, logic down. I think that's a big lesson I learned from working with men.

My entrepreneurship journey was not an easy climb, but worth every painful moment. It was probably the most interesting climb of my life. So many ups and downs. Making money, having no money. Being successful, having no success. Being loved and wanted, and being rejected and not liked. I learned to avoid getting attached to the outcome. I learned to have faith and just keep going. My strong determination, consistency, focus on my goal, clarity on my why, and passion always got me what I wanted.

I hated every step, and I loved every step.

I'm still on my path as an entrepreneur; the path of fulfillment is all that really matters. No mountain is too high to overcome when you can change lives for the better. The lives I touch in this lifetime are my legacy. I'm ready for my next mountain. It forces me to grow and keep getting better and better every single day.

Relationships can feel like hills to walk or mountains to climb. When you're in the right friendships and love relationship, you walk the meadows, hills, and mountains together. You will be there every day, all day, 365 days a year no matter what, whatever it takes. That doesn't mean it's always easy. It's sometimes freaking ugly, and that makes the beautiful moments so amazing. When we're in love, we feel like we're on the mountaintop and we can conquer the world.

And then sometimes we fight and disagree. The same in our friendships. Good relationships are not about how much time we spend together or how often we see each other. They're about the quality of the time we spend together. I have great friendships of thirty-five years in the Netherlands. I only see those friends once a year, but it always feels like I saw them yesterday. I know when I show up spontaneously or in an emergency, there will be a bed for me. I have friends all over the US. When I see them, we have fun and enjoy each other.

I have a very simple rule—when you suck my energy or you're negative, then we have reached our friendship's expiration date. And that's okay. We all have our own path. We're in each other's lives for a reason, a season, or a lifetime. I release in love and gratitude. Friends are chosen.

The family mountain is one of the hardest to climb in my opinion. Family is given to us. My childhood felt like one Mount Everest after another. We're all very different, and I wanted to climb different mountains than my family. Sometimes you come to mountains you need to climb before you can get to the ones you want to climb. However painful some mountains are, the view and perspective when you reach the top are always worth it. You can overcome anything if you choose to. I love my family. I'm grateful for the lessons I learned and the path I had to walk to become who I am today. It was not an easy climb, but it was worth my time and energy. And it will always be worth it.

> *"Climb every mountain until you find your dream, your passion, your true talents, and your happiness. This dream needs all the love you can give, every day for the rest of your life."*
>
> — Esther Wildenberg

LESSONS LEARNED

The hardest mountain to climb is the one within. Mountains are only a problem when they are bigger than you. You should develop yourself so much you become bigger than the mountains you face. Only at the top of a mountain will you meet other leaders who had to climb the same mountains. No landscape inspires quite like the mountains. Mountains just have that alluring quality, and climbing to the top can teach you a lot about life. Dream of the summit and focus on the success of getting to the top. You'll realize afterward that the most profound part was the journey and the effort needed to get there. Success requires effort, perseverance, and the determination to keep pushing yourself, just like climbing a mountain!

> *"You never climb the same mountain twice, not even in memory. Memory rebuilds the mountain, changes the weather, retells the jokes, remakes all the moves."*
>
> — Winston Churchill

Summiting Mount Everest, for example, takes months (if not years) of planning, intensive training, and acclimation. Once the preparation is done, there's still a grueling 29,000-foot vertical climb to the peak. Like climbing Everest, transforming a company doesn't happen overnight; it's done one step at a time. And even with the right preparation and planning, you need to stay focused to survive the inevitable crevasses and avalanches that threaten to knock you and your team off course.

Whether you're gearing up for a business turnaround, meteoric growth, or digital transformation, you're facing big challenges and changes that often come very fast. That is the norm in our digital era. What once took months or years now happens in days or even seconds. Keeping your business ahead of these changes can easily start to feel overwhelming.

To lead and climb successfully, you must be able to visualize success and failure. Have a clear vision for the future. Have the unrelenting belief that you will succeed. Visualize your destination and communicate it to your team. Ensure your team is crystal clear on what ultimate success looks like and what roles they will play in achieving it. Leaders must also ensure their teams are prepared for things that can go wrong by helping them practice the appropriate responses before failures become catastrophic.

Visualizing where you are going is the first step, but determining your path is equally important. Great leaders have a playbook outlining step-by-step execution. Find your accountability partner; they will give you the confidence to push and climb higher. Make sure you're prepared, equipped, and ready.

Build your A Team—a group of like-minded, driven, faithful, loyal, positive, fun people who offer no excuses or reasons to have an excuse. Surround yourself with a group of people who love you, support you, are excited for you, and have an abundance mindset about money, energy, and people. Collaborate, give and take, inspire, and empower. For an A Team to function optimally requires flexibility as much as it does strength. Your story will someday become part of your legacy and will inspire others to climb their own seemingly insurmountable mountains.

EXERCISE

Reflect on the questions below. Then describe how you feel and what actions you could take.

1. What felt like a big mountain?

_____
_____
_____

2. What is your next big mountain to climb? In life? In business? In relationships? In health? In your legacy?

_____
_____
_____
_____
_____
_____
_____
_____

CLIMBING THE MOUNTAIN

3. Which five people will support you on your climb and in the valley?

_____
_____
_____
_____
_____

4. Who do you have to become to climb the mountain and enjoy the view?

_____
_____
_____
_____

5. How would you feel if there were no more mountains to climb?

_____
_____

FIVE TIPS FOR LOVING EVERY MOUNTAIN YOU CLIMB

1. Take a step back now and then; every mountain was huge before you started.
2. When you reach the top, you will never regret the climb.
3. Remove anyone who doesn't support you from your mountain view.
4. Look for the beauty in the climb, just take one step at a time, and breathe.
5. Don't let anyone push you; it's important to rest. It's not a competition.

SUMMARY

We all have mountains to climb. I learned tackling seemingly insurmountable mountains is not as hard as we might think. It just takes a new perspective. If you are currently tackling a mountain that seems way too hard to climb, stand back and look at the big picture. Standing right in front of our challenges, our view is skewed and crowded with the only thing we can see—the mountain.

Tackle your mountains by changing your focus. Focus on the view. Beauty is all around us—even as we're climbing our mountains. Make the intentional decision to focus on those beautiful things. And let go of negative self-talk. Don't doubt your abilities. Once you change to a "Yes, I can!" mindset, you will find hard things become much, much easier. Overcoming challenges really is about mind over matter.

Find someone to enjoy the journey with. Put one foot in front of the other. When you think through each step, you are more likely to take the right first step. Rest is an important part of every journey. Climbing mountains takes energy; we need to allow ourselves time to rest so we can renew that energy and keep moving forward.

> *"If you're serious about changing your life, you'll find a way. If you're not, you'll find an excuse."*
>
> — Jen Sincero

Life is full of challenges. Whatever mountain you face, know you can do hard things. I believe in you. The trick to successfully tackling any mountain is to believe in yourself. Climbing mountains isn't easy. But I guarantee, when you reach the summit, the climb will be worth every step. Once you finally make it to the top, you will be rewarded with a spectacular view. Nothing can compare to the feeling you get as you take in the view. Standing there, on top of the world, enveloped in the magnitude of the view, your heart skips a beat, and you find yourself wishing the moment could last forever. The feeling of accomplishment sweeps over you as you realize you have just conquered a mountain.

We have to climb many mountains. Some are small, but some are huge. But our God is so good, always right beside us as we climb our mountains. Maybe you're in the middle of climbing a mountain right now. It can seem hard, even impossible. It's tempting to give up. But if you turn around, life is all downhill. Giving up is easy, but if we don't persevere and get to the top of the mountain, we will miss out on the blessings God has waiting for us at the top.

"Just because your path is different doesn't mean you're lost."

— Gerard Abrams

CALL TO ACTION

Be grateful for every mountain in your path. Find the right people to climb with. Embrace every mountain because they make you who you are. Stop being comfortable sitting in a mountain meadow. Take the first step on your next big climb today.

Chapter 6

Your Divine Right

"You have a divine right to abundance, and if you are anything less than a millionaire, you haven't had your fair share."

— Stuart Wilde

Do you want to be successful? Do you doubt you will be successful? When would you feel successful? Do you believe prosperity is your divine right? What does divine right mean for you? What does prosperity mean for you, and are you willing to change your thinking to achieve it?

MY STORY

Growing up in a family with a narrow mindset, it wasn't always easy to speak up for my dreams. I believed the family I was born into meant I would live the same life as they did. It's hard when you hear over and over, "When you're a penny, you'll never be a quarter." Who says I was born a penny? Maybe I was a quarter.

"Money doesn't grow on trees." I never even wondered if money grew on trees. All I knew was bills are made from paper, and paper comes from trees. But, of course, that is not what the saying means. Although

I grew up middle class, I had a lot of friends with more money. They lived in beautiful homes, their parents drove expensive cars, and they had a lot of nice clothes and stuff. I played field hockey with these friends and hung out at their homes. I loved being inside those big homes with big yards.

As a teenager, I babysat for a family with four children. They lived in a rich neighborhood next to my high school. I spent a lot of time with them, even when I was not babysitting. I knew back then I wanted to succeed financially, not just in my relationships and health. They were people who just had more education, higher-paying jobs, and maybe even made some good financial investments.

Some came from money, but that's a different story.

I even rode my bicycle home by a different route to see the big homes, nice neighborhoods, and luxury cars. The people were dressed in expensive clothes and somehow inspired me to achieve more. I didn't know how, but I knew why I wanted it. When they say, "Money doesn't buy you happiness," it's true, but it can make life a lot easier, which often leads to happiness—less stress, more self-care, etc.

I had to work hard on my money mindset, my ideas about success, and the vision I had for my life. I searched for a long time—like most of us do. In my thirties, I decided to become an entrepreneur so I would have more freedom and the opportunity to make more money than having a job. Although I had a great career and made a great living, I still wanted more. I was motivated to make a lot of money so I could travel the world and give generously to others. I love to treat people, and I'm all about giving to charities and foundations, especially related to children and dogs.

I was personally developed enough to know I could become anyone and anything I wanted as long as I did the work. I worked many hours and always tried to get better at what I did and how I presented myself while doing it. I believe I went the extra mile and overdelivered most of the time. The downside was my overachievement was not always fulfilling or properly compensated. And I noticed some jealousy from peers and even close friends and family. I never felt I was better than anyone else. I just had different dreams, and my focused drive was not always received well in my environment. It hurt my heart many times, but it didn't stop me.

> *"If you want to live a life you've never lived;*
> *you must do things you've never done."*
>
> — Unknown

Right before I turned forty, I moved to the United States of America—the land of opportunity. I soon realized you could never make the money you can make in America in the Netherlands.

Let me be clear. I have always been ambitious, and I like working. I liked the life I saw in the big houses when I was a kid, but the money wasn't the goal; the money was the means. I wanted to share nice things with those around me and give to the causes and people I hold dear. I believe money and success are energy, and they will flow abundantly when you're aligned with your life purpose and take the action required to fulfill your mission. My money drive was about being able to see as many countries as possible, meet as many people as I could, and explore cultures, food, and languages.

The success I have today is because of who I *had* to become. It's a combination of life choices, preparation, opportunity, hard work, and a little bit of luck.

And I believe I'm just getting started. There's so much work to do in this world; it fuels my need to succeed in every area to create a happy, healthy, and wealthy life for my family and leave a legacy for the next generation and many to come.

"Your achievements are not only due to personal effort and achievements, but also a result of a Higher Power or destiny, claiming a 'right' to success based on divine alignment."

— Esther Wildenberg

LESSONS LEARNED

Everyone has the divine right to be successful. We all get a chance to accomplish that. Success is different for everyone, with no right or wrong. Success is not a simple matter; it cannot be determined merely by the money or material possessions we have. The essence of success goes far deeper. It can only be measured by the extent to which it enhances our inner peace and mental control, enabling us to be happy under all circumstances. That is real success.

The secret of success and happiness is inside you. If you have found success and prosperity outside, but not inside, you are not truly successful. A millionaire who is not happy is not successful. Rich or poor, if your life brings you happiness, you have real success.

A season of failure is the best time to sow the seeds of success. The bludgeon of circumstances may bruise you, but keep your head up. Always try once more, no matter how many times you have failed. Fight when you think you can fight no longer, or when you think you have already done your best, or until your efforts are crowned with success.

Most people only focus about one-tenth of their attention on succeeding. That is why they don't succeed. Do everything using the power of attention. The full force of focused power can be attained through meditation. When you use the focusing power of God or the Divine, you can place it on anything and be a success. Tune yourself into the creative power of Spirit. You will be in contact with the Infinite Intelligence, which can guide you and solve any problems that come up. Power from the dynamic Source of your being will flow uninterrupted so you will be able to perform creatively in any sphere of activity.

"If we suddenly become successful almost effortlessly, then people are envious. It really annoys them that we didn't have to go through all kinds of anguish, pain, and suffering to get there. Their mind believes that such anguish is the cost that must be paid for success."

— David R. Hawkins

I do believe that telling yourself, "Prosperity and success are my divine right," is the key to bringing riches, success, health, and abundance into your life. The word "prosper" means "to succeed, flourish, grow strong and healthy, make successful." Prosperity can have different meanings to people, such as health, wealth, happiness, wonderful experiences, and positive connections. If you are willing to adopt prosperous thinking, you will achieve prosperous results. The Universe is, after all, full of abundance, and it's yours for the taking. This abundance is all around you, as well as within you in the form of your very own talents and abilities. However, you must believe you are worthy of receiving prosperity. Your attitudes, beliefs, ideas, and thoughts are your link with life's abundance and your access to it.

Whatever you radiate outwards in thoughts and feelings—the words you say to yourself, and the pictures you make in your head—affect the prosperity you attract. In his timeless classic *Think and Grow Rich*, Napoleon Hill said, "The subconscious mind works day and night." Hill talks about the power of autosuggestion, which is basically the words you say to yourself. He says, "No thought, whether it be negative or positive, can enter the subconscious mind without the aid of the principle of autosuggestion."

> *"Your mind responds to the pictures you construct and the words you tell yourself."*
>
> — Marisa Peer

Therefore, it makes sense that by speaking, thinking, and even feeling prosperous thoughts, you will attract good fortune. This concept may sound simplistic, but why not try it for yourself?

EXERCISE

Reflect on the questions below. Describe how you feel and what actions you can take.

1. Start your morning routine with visualization, meditation, and affirmations. Write the top three statements you will read out loud for the next thirty days.

   _____
   _____
   _____

2. Write a statement, sentence, or paragraph describing the prosperity you would like to attract.

   _____
   _____
   _____
   _____
   _____
   _____

3. Make a mood board with pictures and quotes that really resonate with you. Write the topics for your vision board here.

   _____
   _____
   _____
   _____

4. What do you believe your divine right is?

_____
_____
_____
_____
_____

FIVE TIPS FOR STARTING TO LIVE YOUR DIVINE SUCCESSFUL LIFE NOW

1. Do everything with the power of attention. What you focus on grows.
2. Be grateful for everything that you have, that you know, and that you've accomplished so far.
3. Live your passion and give first; success will come to you.
4. Don't wait. Success loves speed in taking massive action on your dreams.
5. Claim your divine right to be successful now.

SUMMARY

You have everything it takes to be successful. But you can only fulfill your divine right when you take massive action, when you show the divine you really desire it. Achievements through your and others' efforts should be seen as rent. And it's a rent that must be paid to ensure you keep your eyes on the prize of success.

Often, I see entrepreneurs, business owners, and firms both large and small become successful and then slowly fade away to become also-rans, or worse still, end up fighting for their very existence. In almost all cases, they have become distracted from the prize that comes from executing a profitable business plan. Distraction takes many forms; surprisingly, it can frequently be traced back to earlier success—they believed it was a divine right and forgot to pay the rent daily in effort. Focusing on the prize requires focus, determination, resilience, passion, action, faith, patience, and consistency. Divine right is not luck; it's connecting and aligning with the Divine and doing the work to make it a fulfilling achievement.

> *"The strongest single factor in prosperity consciousness is self-esteem: believing you deserve it, believing you will get it."*
>
> — Jerry Gillies

For the next ninety days, read your prosperity statement out loud; think it in your head, feel it in your being, and make it part of your everyday life. Do this constantly and consistently and you will receive it all.

Here are some statements to get you started: "Prosperity is my divine right. Success is my divine right. I am wealthy, inside and out. My income is increasing; I prosper wherever I turn. I deserve the best, and I accept the best now. This is a rich Universe, and there is plenty for us all. The more I prosper, the more I must share with everyone else. I am rich, I am healthy, and I am happy. The Universe always provides. I give thanks now for all the good I have and all the good things to come. I am one with the Universal power of abundance and prosperity, and I am always provided for beyond my needs. I am independently happy, wealthy, and healthy. It is easy for me to receive massive wealth."

Align with these statements and they can all become your truth. Divine right is the alignment between what you want and the actions you take, the choices you make, and the attention you give.

Fulfillment is a success, but success is not fulfillment. Achievements outside fulfillment are not true success. Ask the Divine Source to show you the Divine definition of your existence because that's where your true success and fulfillment lies. A person may succeed, but that doesn't mean fulfillment. Fulfillment is the achievement of your purpose of existence. Maybe the better statement is: It's your divine right to live a fulfilled life.

"God has perfect timing; never early, never late. It takes a little patience, and it takes a lot of faith, but it's worth the wait."

— Unknown

CALL TO ACTION

Define success. Act on your desire to be successful. Align your attention with what fulfills you. Do things you have never done. And watch what happens. Become the person you're destined to be.

Chapter 7

Be a World Traveler

"Twenty years from now you will be more disappointed by the things that you didn't do than by the ones you did do. So, throw off the bowlines. Sail away from the safe harbor. Catch the trade winds in your sails. Explore. Dream. Travel. Discover."

— Author Unknown

Do you have the traits of a world traveler? Are you looking to become a better person, traveler, or citizen of the world? Have you ever experienced culture shock? Do you know the power of being a world traveler? Are you a student of the world?

MY STORY

As a child I traveled with my parents and two sisters mainly to France, Germany, and Belgium. They were comfortable places for my parents to drive to. We went to the same places for several years. My parents didn't like change much. Knowing what to expect is safe. As a child, I didn't know this was so limiting, but when I turned sixteen, I went with friends on an airplane to Spain, and so the trouble began.

I was not the most confident teenager, so I followed my girlfriends wherever they wanted to go. At sixteen, I was aware of the danger six young girls faced walking late at night in the streets of Marbella. We agreed to always stay together, but as you can guess, that didn't happen. And suddenly, we were short one friend. She went with a boy to his apartment.

Later, we learned she was okay, but we spent a few scary hours awake and waiting for her to come back to our hotel. She showed up at 6 a.m. That was my first lesson in dealing with fear and understanding the power of sticking to your word when traveling with a group. She had a great night, but the rest of us had a horrible one.

I always loved traveling, alone or with others. I liked my girls' trips to Spain, Ibiza, Mallorca, Crete, Zakynthos, Lesvos, and Kos. At nineteen, I went on my first ski vacation to Austria with my friends. I was sold. Skiing was my new favorite vacation. Skiing in France, Switzerland, and Austria was a lot of fun, especially the apres-ski parties.

In my twenties, I went skiing with friends and coworkers at least twice a year. I believe some people still know my name in St. Anton, Austria. Those ski weeks were a blast, and I have incredible memories from those years.

In my early twenties (before my accident), I went to Florida to visit my twin sister Nicole. She worked at the Grand Floridian at Disney World. My cousin and I rented a car and traveled the state, seeing the Florida Keys, the Everglades, and all the great beaches. It was my first trip outside of Europe. I was sold on traveling more outside of Europe, and so my world travel journey had begun.

I started my travel bucket list, and the list got longer and longer. The United States was not really on it, so Florida was my only trip there. My mantra became: I will work hard so I can be a world traveler. It takes a lot of money to see the world. The cheapest way to travel was backpacking, so I bought all my gear, and the adventures started right after my recovery at twenty-seven.

> *"Once a year, go someplace you've never been before."*
>
> — Dalai Lama

Later, but while I was still young, I went to Guatemala, Belize, Honduras, and Mexico. I went with a friend, which I thought was a great idea. Then, we had a three-day layover in New York. After exploring the city and staying at a youth hostel, my friend fell in love with a girl, and before I knew it, I was on my own traveling to South America. Looking back, it was not the smartest idea. I felt unsafe, and I was scared. I didn't run from the fear; I sat with it. I let the fear change me into someone who feels fear but travels anyway.

I spent some time learning the difference between healthy fear and an intuition that something was "off" or "wrong." As a rule, if the idea of something fills you with 50 percent fear and 50 percent excitement, it's probably the good type of fear.

After my adventures in Honduras, I traveled by bus to Guatemala, which was not a fun experience. I arrived in Guatemala City in the middle of the night and on the wrong side of the city. It was one of my scariest moments ever. I stopped a taxi, praying the driver wouldn't kill me. I asked him to take me to the airport. He did. When I arrived at the airport, it was closed. I couldn't stay at the airport, so I went to a hotel next to it. They had a room.

As soon as I could, I called my airline to book a ticket home on the first available flight. The first flight left at 9 a.m. I stayed awake, counting the minutes to check in and getting out of this nightmare. I called my dad and his girlfriend to pick me up at the airport when I got home. I never felt so happy as the moment I landed at Schiphol Airport, Amsterdam.

But I didn't let that experience stop me. I was excited to go to Asia. At twenty-nine, I met my girlfriend Aletta, and we booked our first vacation together to Thailand, Laos, and Cambodia. We flew to Bangkok and traveled by foot, bus, tuk tuk, and train. We stayed at cheap hotels and even slept on the beach. I loved the backpacking lifestyle. We booked a room for the first night in Bangkok, and for the rest of the three weeks, we just let the journey take us where we were meant to go. This way of traveling with just the *Lonely Planet* and speaking with your hands and feet to get rides or directions was fun. Because we had no plan and didn't know where we were going, we ended up in the most amazing places. We met other backpackers from around the world and sat around campfires on the beach, having great conversations and dancing until late in the night. We stared at the stars and made wishes. We shared food and exchanged contact information with people we met. My free spirit absolutely loved these trips.

A year later, Aletta and I went back to Thailand to explore more by train, seeing the south of Thailand. This time we planned a few stops, but we still didn't lock anything in. We flew to Bangkok and took the train to the south of Thailand, close to the border of Malaysia. It was December 2004. Remember the tsunami on December 26 that year? That event changed so many lives around the world, including mine. Days before the tsunami, we were on the beach when I had this weird feeling something was going to happen. I had to assess whether it was fear or excitement. I knew in my gut it was fear, but I couldn't explain what it was. Our train was not leaving for two more days, but I wanted to leave right then. After Aletta and I fought for hours about leaving, we left. I was going with or without her.

We arrived at the train station, hoping there were two seats for us. But there were none. The only spot they had was between the goats and chickens. I said, "I'll take it." Aletta thought I was crazy because two days later we had tickets for a private cabin. For twelve hours, she moaned while I tried to sleep in the goat pee and poo.

When we finally arrived in Bangkok, the silence between us was louder than words. She was mad as hell. We found a nice hotel, took a shower, and turned on the television.

The tsunami had just hit Thailand—the beach we had been on the day before was gone.

Friends we met on our trip were still there. We didn't hear from them until we had been home for two weeks. Fortunately, we were all alive and had incredible memories and life lessons.

Every year, I travel for business and pleasure. Cheri, Kai, and I go back to the Netherlands as a family to see my friends and family and enjoy my home country. You can take this girl out of the Netherlands, but you can't take being Dutch out of me. I always get the feeling of coming home, although my home is now the United States, and I won't move back to the Netherlands.

In 2020, our travel and life changed. In 2020, travel was limited, but we did everything we could to travel anyway. Kai was born in May, and in November, we were on a plane to Florida. When Kai turned one, we flew to the Netherlands and Kai became a world traveler, getting his first stamp in his passport.

The next summer, we spent five weeks in Italy and the Netherlands. Traveling with a toddler is not for the faint of heart. We had an amazing time in Florence, with lots of day trips, and Kai loved his pizza and gelato. We decided to take him everywhere, from vineyards to visiting little villages, having delicious meals, and hanging out at the pool. Traveling makes you richer as a soul, even when it's harder with a child. But watching him glow and be so happy getting his first kiss at three years old at the playground in Italy made it worth every tough moment.

I have traveled to incredible places around the world. I have been to all continents except Antarctica—that will happen in the next few years. I can share beautiful and amazing stories of all my trips. I have traveled to sixty countries. That's still only one fourth of the world. In my trips, from backpacking, sleeping in hostels, renting apartments and villas, to five-star spas and resorts, the best memories were always a combination of who I was traveling with, sharing that unique moment, and being one with the place I was in. Every trip was a unique experience, and I have hundreds, if not thousands of very special memories. All my travel with friends, family, partners, and business colleagues has been worth every minute, especially the seventy-five retreats and masterminds I have hosted around the world, which are in my special memory bank. When you travel and transform lives at the same time, it's not just an adventure; it's impact, legacy, and fulfillment at another level.

> *"The more places I see and experience, the more I realize the world has so much beauty. The more I become aware of it, the more I realize how relatively little I know, how many places I still have to go, how much more there is to learn, and how much more there is to love."*
>
> — Esther Wildenberg

LESSONS LEARNED

You can be a world traveler even if you haven't been to every continent or every country or even if you've only left the US once. Being a world traveler is all about your mindset and being curious. That is what you cultivate both at home and abroad. When you travel, you get to know the world. You get to see how people move through different cities, how they go on with their lives despite obstacles, and how different countries interact with each other. The more you travel, the more you see your own country differently. My travels contextualize the US, so it starts to feel like a huge place with people who spend most of their lives inside its borders. There are many people who barely leave the state where they're born, even though there's a whole wide world waiting to welcome them!

Your mission on this giant floating rock is to learn, grow, and investigate the planet like you're writing a thesis on it. Be more curious. You don't need to know everything upfront. It's not about studying the *Lonely Planet* books or endless research on Google. As I child, you were born with extreme curiosity. Now that I have my four-year-old son, I see the world through his eyes and his curiosity. It's great to recognize I never lost my curiosity. If you have lost yours, find it and start exploring. Stoke the flames inside you. Feed them with all the things that hold your attention and pique your interest. Don't judge your interests; just follow them. For me, one of the joys of traveling is seeing people live in their authentic place and wondering what their daily life looks like. I love seeing the world's natural wonders, tasting the local food, listening to the sound of different languages, and experiencing the magic of each culture.

> *"Travel is about the gorgeous feeling of teetering in the unknown."*
>
> — Anthony Bourdain

A sense of wonder at the unknown is one of the greatest gifts of being alive; don't squander it by judging your own curiosity. When you've finished your travels and are heading home, bring the curiosity with you. Cultivate a sense of wonder that never leaves you, that drives you to ask questions about the world and read books and listen to the voices of people in faraway lands. You don't even have to say the thoughts out loud, although doing so might help you attract similar-minded investigative ponderers of the universe.

You meet the most amazing people when you travel. Travel is a form of education. Traveling is the best personal development opportunity. I am who I am today because I have been to sixty countries and many more are on my bucket list. I live to travel; I love exploring the world. It makes me feel like the richest person ever.

I'm surrounded by entrepreneurs and business owners who love to travel the world. You find yourself in very different conversations when you're a world traveler. The more you learn, the richer life becomes. Be a student of the world, one who learns because they know that life is both punishingly short and infinitely interesting, if you just know how to listen. Every place you visit has a context. Every person you meet has a story. Every story has a context. Piece the world together for yourself as if each story, person, and context throughout history were a precious puzzle piece presented just to you. Everything has a reason. The world is yours; walk it intentionally.

"The world is a book and those who do not travel read only one page."

— Augustine of Hippo

The more you travel, the more experience you'll have with fear. You'll start to learn the difference between merely unfamiliar situations and the unusual, dangerous, or life-threatening. Sit with the newness and replace it with adventure. Fear and excitement are the energy, the same feeling, the same movement in your body. Traveling makes you more resilient, more confident, and all around happy and grateful. All world travelers learn to adapt. Adapting when you're traveling often looks like changing your behavior to better fit the cultural context you're in. Remember, you, as a traveler, are entering someone else's culture, and it is likely to be different from what you are used to. Things that are perfectly acceptable at home might be considered extremely rude abroad. It's your job to do as few of those things as you can while on your trip.

My goal is to try my hand at living like a citizen of the place I'm visiting, at least as much as I can. If you get culture shock, know that it passes. Culture shock can sometimes present as anger or frustration at a place where the customs, manners, foods, and sounds start to sound irritating and unreasonable. But remember, it's all in your perspective.

When you focus on growing, exploring, and being curious, travel is a beautiful way to spend time because it helps your brain stretch, grow, learn, and adapt in ways that aren't necessary at home. Travel asks us to chart our path, make decisions with unknown variables, depend on complete strangers, and collaborate with all the moving mechanisms of a new place. A novice traveler might try to bend the place to their will instead of practicing acceptance and adapting. As you travel more, and travel better, allow yourself to change. Be changed by the places you visit, the people you meet, the food you eat, and the times you find little sparks of beauty in the world.

Find the joy in exploration, in seeing something anew, in seeing yourself as a different person than the one you once recognized. And show yourself you can, in fact, be better, more compassionate, less stuck in your ways, and more loving.

Travel can also teach us boundaries, to look out for ourselves, and to know not everyone means well. For all the good, joy, and light in the world, there are also those who will take advantage, cause harm, or take, but travel helps you to be better attuned to that energy.

> *"Live life with no excuses, travel with no regret."*
>
> — Oscar Wilde

World travelers are always growing, often in ways they never expected. They're improving their navigation skills, developing communication skills, managing fear, and learning about the world. If you want to be a world traveler, start by asking yourself, "What can I learn from this?" or "How can I be better by doing this?" whenever you have the opportunity. Know that "I've always done it this way" is not a good reason, on its face, to continue to do that thing. If a better way comes along, take it!

If you're willing to change, to adapt, and accept there's almost always a better way to do something, you'll be well on your way to cultivating a world traveler mindset. Travel helps you understand the world is so wonderfully, unapologetically large, filled with people who are like you in some ways, but very different in others. The world has people everywhere who want to make it a better place, filling their days with little plans to bring lightness, joy, and smiles to the people around them.

Become a world traveler by connecting. Connect with places, with people, with cultures, with landscapes; let travel teach you that you're part of the world and there's always a place for you. Connection and belonging are intrinsically intertwined—to connect with others is to know you belong. You are the world.

"Traveling—it leaves you speechless, then turns you into a storyteller."

— Ibn Battuta

EXERCISE

Think about the prompts below and describe how you feel and what actions you could take.

1. How many countries have you visited? Which one was your favorite and why?

_____
_____
_____

2. Write a declaration to yourself to encourage your curiosity to travel more.

   _____
   _____
   _____

3. Join travel groups on social media. Do you like to meet new people who inspire you to travel?

   _____
   _____
   _____
   _____

4. What do you need to change to become a world traveler?

   _____
   _____
   _____
   _____

5. Make a picture board with images from the countries and places you'd like to go. Are you ready to become a world traveler? If yes, what action can you take now to make that happen? If not, what would it take to get you there?

   _____
   _____
   _____
   _____
   _____
   _____

FIVE TIPS FOR BECOMING A WORLD TRAVELER

1. Change your mindset to see you are already a traveler.

2. Describe the ideal group of people to travel with.

3. Make a top ten list of countries you'd like to visit and make a timeline to travel to them.

4. Join travel groups. Read travel books. Be curious.

5. Book your next trip now. Start planning now. You only have now.

SUMMARY

If your goal is to become a world traveler, just do it. Don't wait until retirement to see the beauty of this world. Traveling will make you feel like the richest person. When you do travel, be kind to yourself. Look around. Take in the scenery. Be present because presence is what it means to be alive. Be forever looking for context and love, intrigue, and delicious food. Try things you don't normally try. Be open to experiences. Take some healthy risks. Meet people and ask them about themselves. You only learn by experiencing new things. Travel takes courage. It takes the courage to be uncomfortable. It takes courage to be in a new place, around new people. It takes courage to try new things and continue to try new things even when you're not sure if you're doing it right. I know you have this courage, and you can continue to cultivate it on every trip you take, near and far.

As a world traveler, you don't need to visit 101 countries, all the oceans, or all the continents. Just visit as many countries as you desire. I encourage you to circumnavigate the world, east to west. See a variety of terrains like the desert, tundra, steppe, rainforest, white sandy beaches, mountains, waterfalls, caves, hot springs, and glaciers. Travel by car, bicycle, train, ship, camel, yacht, motorcycle, bus, or on foot. Become familiar with many cultures, religions, traditions, languages, food, people, and extremes.

> *"We live in a wonderful world that is full of beauty, charm, and adventure. There is no end to the adventures we can have if only we seek them with our eyes open."*
>
> — Jawaharial Nehru

CALL TO ACTION

The world is your playground. Explore outside your state and country. Spend more money on experiences and less on stuff. Start making your top ten list of countries you want to visit. I challenge you to see how much the world has to offer in so many ways. Book your dream trip now; don't wait for the perfect time.

Chapter 8

Deepen Your Leadership

"A leader is great, not because of his or her power, but because of his or her ability to empower others."

— John Maxwell

If you wouldn't follow yourself, why should anyone else? Are you a leader worth following? Why? Are you building to last? How? Which skill needs the most improvement—competency, commitment, or character? Do your time investments at work reflect how you want to lead? Are you interested in trying to be interesting, or are you committed to being a leader in your industry and mastering it? Are you the leader of the future? Let me share my story of how I became a leader.

MY STORY

I'm extremely passionate about world-class leadership and becoming an empowered leader. Why? We all have examples of bad managers, bosses, leaders, and executives. I could write a book on that topic alone. My career started early. I had my first summer job at fourteen, cleaning older people's homes. The only reason I did it was it paid well, but I only did it one summer. Several summers I worked at beach clubs, serving the tourists who were sunbathing. I would walk through the sand to serve them cold drinks and delicious food. My first ugly experience with a boss happened when a group of German men ran away without paying their bill. My boss said, "We will deduct that from your pay at the end of the day," and he did. I quit and went to work at the competition next door. Lesson learned. At the new beach club, I asked people to pay right away, and I always made them feel good. I nearly walked off the legs from under my body, but I made a lot of money, great tips, got a nice tan, and lost weight.

As a teenager, I had several jobs. At seventeen, I started working at a fresh bread and pastry bakery. Those were long days from 6 a.m. to 6 p.m. I had a very lovely manager and a very kind boss. I worked there five years every Saturday and on holidays and breaks. When I finished my studies at the University of Amsterdam, I started working full-time as a dental hygienist and children's dentist. I worked for three different offices, and then I started my own. My experience was not glorious; the work was stressful, and I didn't like it. I realized I was not really made to work for someone. The lack of great communication, lack of emotional intelligence, lack of management, and lack of positivity almost killed me. I had one wonderful boss; she owned a big dental office in The Hague. She was positive, generous, flexible, and gave me the freedom to be me and do me. When she sold her successful business, I left. She was my first experience of a great leader, not just a boss or manager, and she was an incredible leader! As I shared earlier, my dental career ended when I was twenty-three because of my accident and long rehab time. I was never sad that I couldn't go back to the dental industry.

During the last year of my recovery, I worked part time at a lunchroom in The Hague. The owners were a powerful couple. I enjoyed working for them, and I loved the service industry. They were great leaders; they felt more like family than my bosses. They were warm, friendly, generous, and grateful for my hard work. They gave me responsibility and leadership to run the business when they were gone. I learned a lot about honesty, integrity, hard work, kindness, over-delivering, and money.

After my three-year break of recovery, rehab, personal development, and thinking about my next move in life, I was invited to work in the fitness industry. I had played sports my whole life, and during my recovery time, I had a personal trainer, so I decided it would be a great fit. The fitness industry was a happy place for me. I enjoyed working for four big giants in the industry in the Netherlands. My career advanced from salesperson to sales manager, then general manager, and finally vice president and opening new locations in the Benelux. I learned a lot about business, finding opportunities, hiring and firing people, communication, and managing dynamics. I experienced great leadership and bad management, manipulation, liars, and jealousy. I had my first experience getting hurt because I was more successful than the men around me. Then I quit my job and took a month off to apply for a brand-new opportunity.

Realizing I had never really had to apply for a job or compete with other candidates, I was up for a new challenge. I wrote my resume and put it online with a recruiting agency—a new world for me. I crossed my fingers and hoped for an amazing job. The next day, I received an email inviting me to a phone interview. The recruiting agency's owner called me personally to learn more about me and the story behind my weird resume. It had no logic or sequence because of all the hoops and jumps I had made so far, including my three-year break in my early twenties. She was impressed with my background, rehab, determination, willpower, commitment, and passion to succeed. She introduced me to the company owner, who hired me based on my values and beliefs rather than my resume. The company owner became my mentor and role model throughout my career, and even today, I refer to her a lot. She inspired me to become the best I could be by doing the work, listening, overdelivering, and inspiring people.

My whole career I mostly worked with men, egos, and wannabes. The corporate world is an interesting environment. Although I was successful in corporate, it was not the environment I was meant to be in full-time. I love consulting with C-suite executives because I like to push them out of their boxes to look with fresh eyes at their businesses. I have seen a lot of environments that model the kinds of leaders I don't want to be. Leadership is a fascinating role in business and life. I always share that leadership is not your title; your title determines your position in the organization so people can find you. Leadership is how you show up, how you treat others, and how you create a way to have people fall in love with your communication, your actions, and how you make them feel. I have met CEOs who are great business owners, but terrible leaders. I have managers who are incredible leaders. I have observed people my whole life, and the best leaders are those who love what they do and spread their love with others so they feel loved. Love makes people work harder, and then they will not leave your company or team. Love is great business. When you touch someone's heart, they will follow you wherever you go.

> *"Be a trailblazer! Do what you feel is right in your heart. They will criticize you but won't forget you."*
> — Esther Wildenberg

LESSONS LEARNED

I was not born a leader. I had to work myself up to being one. From being a follower of followers, to becoming a follower of a leader, to being a leader, and now I'm a leader of leaders. Leadership is an ongoing journey of personal development and business growth. To interact, you must master the art of communicating with people. When you become a people reader and magnet, the world is yours. It's not just who you know, but who knows you. They will remember you because of your charismatic presence, your unique thinking, and your actions.

Leadership changes as fast as everything else is changing. In an era of rapid technological advancements, globalization, and evolving employee expectations, traditional models of leadership are becoming increasingly obsolete. The hierarchical approach, where leaders give directives and subordinates follow, is shifting toward a more decentralized, collaborative paradigm. As organizations confront complex challenges requiring multidimensional solutions, the concept of empowerment becomes key.

Empowered leadership is an advanced form of management where leaders actively enable and encourage team members to take initiative, make decisions, and assume responsibilities. It is built on the pillars of trust, transparency, and shared objectives. Rather than a one-way flow of commands, this model fosters an environment of open dialogue, creative problem-solving, and shared accountability.

In corporations, it means leaders practice empowerment and trust their teams, giving them the autonomy to execute tasks, manage projects, and even make high-stakes decisions without micromanagement. An empowered leader not only communicates the organizational goals clearly, but engages team members in goal-setting processes, ensuring everyone is aligned and motivated. They share their vision. This leadership style creates an atmosphere conducive to continuous learning and development. Feedback is a two-way street, allowing leaders and team members to grow and adapt.

In an empowered setting, decisions are made collectively, leveraging the diverse skills and perspectives within the team. This often leads to innovation and more effective solutions.

Empowered leadership is a strategic imperative for organizations aspiring to thrive in the modern landscape. By focusing on autonomy, shared vision, continuous learning, and collaborative decision-making, leaders can unlock unprecedented performance and job satisfaction among teams. It is the power of vision, core culture values, authenticity, transparency, humility, and gratitude in determining what it means to be a leader.

"I've learned that people will forget what you said, people will forget what you did, but people will never forget how you made them feel."

— Maya Angelou

Leadership in network marketing and in small businesses have the same core values. But it's a little bit more like the Wild, Wild West. Leadership plays a pivotal role in empowering people in these industries. The small business owner, the salesperson, and the single entrepreneur all represent a product or service, either their own or someone else's. When you depend on yourself to make a living, meaning you're not on payroll for a company, leadership has a whole other meaning. In corporations, you can easily get away with being a follower or being invisible. As long as you do the minimum requirements, you will have a job most of the time.

I'm not talking about satisfaction, just leadership. Becoming an empowered leader in the small business world requires ongoing personal development, reading books, attending conferences and summits, and hiring the right mentors and coaches. And all this inner work only works when you use it and apply it in your daily life. We all strive to live free. But life and business will always be team sports. Become the leader you wish you had.

"Before you are a leader, success is all about growing yourself. When you become a leader, success is all about growing others."

— Jack Welch

EXERCISE

Reflect on the questions below and describe how you feel and what actions you can take.

1. What steps can you take next to transform into an empowered leader?

   _____
   _____
   _____

2. In which areas do you need mentorship?

   _____
   _____
   _____

3. Who do you want to be as a leader? What would you like to be known for?

   _____
   _____
   _____
   _____

4. Who is your example of an empowered leader?

   _____
   _____

5. Who would follow you and be your fellow leaders? Which traits, behaviors, and values do they have?

   _____
   _____
   _____
   _____
   _____

FIVE TIPS FOR BECOMING AN EMPOWERED LEADER

1. Commit to being the best leader you can be.

2. Show anyone who says you're not a leader they are wrong.

3. Read leadership books and join leadership events.

4. Surround yourself with great leaders.

5. Start today by leading yourself first. That is step one for an empowered leader.

SUMMARY

Transformational empowered leadership is driven by one's soul purpose, passion, and genuine desire to make lasting change. True leadership is about authenticity, vulnerability, and the ability to inspire and motivate others for the right reasons. Transformational empowered leadership stems from an internal desire to make life better for humanity, not from external recognition or material success. Authenticity and consistency in one's actions build genuine connections and inspire others. Leadership is not confined to title or rank; it's about showing up daily and being a positive influence on others. Energy, passion, and excitement are crucial, especially in a post-COVID world where many feel disconnected or unmotivated. Collaboration, high emotional intelligence, and the ability to inspire growth in others are essential traits of a transformational leader. Aspiring transformational leaders should align with their soul's purpose, share their stories openly, and lead by example to create meaningful and lasting change.

Being a consultant and executive coach for twenty years, I have seen all leadership styles and lack thereof. Leadership is a skillset you can learn. High emotional intelligence is a big driver in becoming an empowered leader. Be someone people want to follow for who you are, not the product you offer. Be so good at what you do that no one can take their eyes off you or ignore you. The market pays for the best. When you leave people better than you found them, you know you did a great job. Always avoid being arrogant or too good for certain people. You will have raving fans, customers, and followers of your work who will buy and do anything you do. And they're all equally important. Empowered leaders are extremely focused. They eliminate distractions and are not attached to what the outside world thinks of them. Remember, failure is greatness yet to happen. Having followers does not make you a leader.

You're an empowered leader worth following when you're committed no matter what. You do the work, show up, and lead in good times and in bad times. When you're interested in doing something, you do it only when circumstances permit.

Commitment keeps you going in the face of adversity and challenges. When you're committed to something, you accept no excuses, only results. Commitment ignites action. Commitment is persistence with purpose. Commitment is respect. Leaders must continually evaluate their commitment to the people they lead and to their purpose.

People follow you because of who you are and what you represent. You're humble, genuine, honest, and coachable. People follow you because of what you have done for the organization. People follow you because of what you have done for them. The goal of leadership is to develop leaders, not gain followers. People follow you because they want to. They follow because you care about them. When you become an empowered leader, you transform your results. Results transform when your culture transforms. Culture transforms when your behavior transforms. Behavior transforms when your mindset transforms. When, as a leader, you commit to developing yourself, you naturally foster a culture of continuous learning—followers/employees will follow your example and embrace growth opportunities. Committed leaders encourage continuous learning.

> *"Let us all be the leaders we wish we had."*
> — Simon Sinek

CALL TO ACTION

List your unique leadership skills. I encourage you to step into being a leader. Work hard, be smart, and lead by example. The world needs you as an empowered leader. I challenge you to start being that future leader now.

*"Leaders aren't born; they are made.
And they are made just like anything else—through hard work."*

— Vince Lombardi

Chapter 9

Healing Your Life

"Turn your hurt into healing, your wounds into wisdom, and your pain into power."

— Robin Sharma

Do you ever ask yourself how your heart is today? Do you wonder what life would be without feeling sad or angry? Are you stuck in the past? How can you be a better version of yourself today? What do you want to pay attention to? Where did you notice beauty today? Healing isn't easy after you've been undermined much of your life until you believe you aren't enough or not deserving of happiness. I want to share how I came to love myself so you can also learn how to heal.

MY STORY

For a long time, I believed I was not good enough. I didn't love myself. I tended toward pleasing people. My thoughts became my reality, and that reality didn't serve me. I was not happy. I didn't grow up with many happy examples. My two near-death experiences and long recovery after an accident were huge wake-up calls, making me think about how I wanted to live my life. I knew I was a kind, loving, funny, positive, and pretty young adult with huge potential for doing anything I wanted to do. But to succeed, I knew I had to start healing my emotional and mental wounds first.

In my late twenties I went to a Louise Hay seminar in the Netherlands. She spoke about thinking positively and constantly reminding yourself to be positive every time you thought or said something to yourself. I started to put yellow sticky notes everywhere in my home and car. I put reminders in my phone, and my alarm was set to go off with a kind message to myself. In the beginning, this practice was funny and weird, but I kept looking at the notes to program myself to look at myself differently, to see myself as more positive, happy, loving, and believing. I wrote: "I love me. I'm smart. I'm good looking. I have a great body. I'm a good friend. I'm sexy. Etc."

> *"Remember, you have been criticizing yourself for years and it hasn't worked. Try approving of yourself and see what happens."*
>
> — Louise Hay

I hired a coach to help me with deep patterns and beliefs. I attended many rebirth, inner child, and family design sessions, plus did one-on-one coaching to undo the painful negative programming from my childhood and young adult life. I spent at least two years with her coaching me to feel confident, happy, and passionate about life.

During my recovery, staying for months in the hospital, I chose to watch Tony Robbins DVDs every day. Right before my accident, I ordered a black box with six CDs I saw on an infomercial. I watched the CDs repeatedly, listening to Robbins' powerful message, healing my heart and optimizing my mindset to get my body back in shape, healthy and stronger than ever before.

After several months, I came home, and I kept listening until I knew what Robbins was going to say. He saved my life. He was my inspiration to keep going, to believe in myself, and to forgive my past, the people who hurt me, and the pain and abuse I had gone through. I have been following Robbins for twenty-six years, and I wished to meet him in person and thank him. In 2017, I met him backstage at a conference. We didn't have a chance to talk, but we took a picture. In 2024, I had the honor of talking to him personally via Zoom. I shared my story and thanked him. I believe in miracles and in divine timing. And I will manifest meeting him in person to have a heart-to-heart conversation.

"People who fail focus on what they have to go through; people who succeed focus on what it will feel like at the end."

— Tony Robbins

In 2013, I met Cheri Tree. She was the only female keynote speaker at an event in Amsterdam with celebrity speakers like Robert Kiyosaki and Les Brown. Her energy, methodology, and determination to help entrepreneurs with the system she created made buying her BANK training a no-brainer. I went to the two-day, in-person training in Amsterdam.

The BANK system healed my heart. I could connect the dots backward to see why I was parented the way I was and why my past relationships hadn't worked out as I dreamed. Looking through my ex-partners' lenses and taking away the judgment was so fulfilling. We're all amazing human beings, and we're all annoying at the same time. The beauty is in the diversity of personality types. I truly love my family, friends, and all my ex-partners. They are all part of my life journey. I don't regret any of my choices, relationships, or adventures.

I studied the BANK CDs for six months straight. Every time I drove, I listened to the same four CDs. They helped me prepare for business meetings, in-person conversations, and in healing my breakup with a partner I deeply loved. It's okay to realize you're not an optimal match and still love each other.

In 2023, Robin Sharma was my mentor. I was part of an elite group of thirty people from around the world. We all met in person in December 2022 in Barcelona. Sitting in an intimate setting with only thirty people and Robin Sharma was an incredible experience. I had read all his books, implemented several of his systems, and deconstructed his principles prior to joining his mastermind.

After the COVID lockdown and having a baby, I needed to be back in a room with successful business professionals. I had been so focused on being a mom, keeping the household going, and supporting Cheri in our company, Codebreaker Technologies, that I had lost my passion for living my purpose and daily creating my legacy. Being a mom is a legacy project. I knew I was here to do more as well, but I lost my connection to my dreams. That week of traveling by myself and focusing on me helped me return to my power, dreams, and passion to create my new path with clarity and determination. I want to be a great example for Kai. Life will throw you curve balls; how fast you can pivot out of them is what matters.

My time with Robin Sharma and thirty friends was incredible. I learned a lot and implemented many of the principles. The most important one was about my health. I wanted to be in the best shape of my adult life when I turned fifty in January 2025. I leveled up my exercise, meditation, outdoor adventures, sauna visits, massages, and natural supplements. My second most important focus is investing in my love relationship and recreating the relationship so it's deeper than it ever was before. I believe when you heal your heart, everything else will fall in place much more easily, like money, relationships, business opportunities, health goals, and having more joy and peace.

In 2024, my wife Cheri and I went to an incredible event hosted by our dear friend, speaker and life coach Danny Morel. His event, Awaken, was focused on healing your heart to transform to your next best level. Cheri and I went together to take a deep dive into some wounds we had acquired over the past few years. It was great to do healing work with my partner. While we each have our own pain and trauma, we had also experienced some together over the past few years as a couple. Personal development and healing your heart is an ongoing journey. We all get hurt a lot. But how we heal, forgive, and move on is what matters. Life is too short to live in the past.

> *"The power of healing lies in healing your heart. When you face your heartbreak and the pain you've imprisoned inside of you, you will feel free, confident, and happy."*
>
> — Esther Wildenberg

LESSONS LEARNED

Success isn't an accident, but it's not luck or talent either. Success is about persistence. It's about having ultimate belief in yourself and finding your inner strength. It's training yourself to get up as fast as you can when you get knocked down and get back in the game of life.

Creating positive change is hard. It is like planting seeds. It takes time for the seeds to sprout, and we need to constantly nurture the seedlings and keep the weeds away. Positive change happens by healing your heart. Your body stores your trauma, emotions, feelings, and thoughts. I had to let go of old beliefs, beliefs I got from my parents, teachers, and friends. What you focus on will grow. We hear that all the time, and it's so true. Habitually thinking in positive affirmations and using the present tense, e.g. "I am," "I have," will really transform you in a positive way.

After doing so much work, I realized the soul, heart, mind, and body are all one. When you exercise, you're more positive and happier. When you eat healthy foods, you feel better and have more energy. When you train your mind with positive affirmations, all that's left is to love yourself for who you are.

Visualizing is a powerful way of creating your dream for your future, happy life. I started journaling in my mid-thirties; it helped me clear my mind to write down my ideas and feelings and catch myself when I became stuck on an old pattern. Meditation is the best way to really connect with your soul, your true self. It allows you to enter into a deep state of gratitude and remember your unique talents and gifts. Another powerful way is prayer. Also helpful is going for a walk in nature by yourself and letting the wind, trees, and all nature's elements speak to you—you'll feel the inner peace.

> *"If you talk about it, it's a dream. If you envision it, it's possible. If you schedule it, it's real."*
>
> — Tony Robbins

How we think and speak leads to our body's "eases" and "dis-eases." We create every dis-ease in our body through our own thought patterns. Essentially, patterns of thought relating to resentment, anger, criticism, guilt, and fear are the main contributors to our so-called illnesses. Forgiveness and releasing these thought patterns alongside healthy nutrition and care for our body are the key to wellness. I have lived by these truths for ten years. I'm a firm believer in holistic healing and that the body can heal itself. If you can create a disease in your body, you can also heal your body.

Actively engaging in forgiveness sessions with yourself or others is very powerful. I personally like to do the Ho'oponopono to forgive myself.

Cheri and I use it a lot in our marriage and even with our four-year-old son. We all make mistakes or say things we don't mean. The key is to catch yourself fast and heal it right away. This mantra for self-love is a beautiful and easy way to forgive yourself and others.

The word Ho'oponopono roughly translates as "to cause things to move back into balance" or "to make things right." It's a very Zen concept. (In native Hawaiian language, "pono" means "balance," in the sense of "life." When things are in balance, nothing is off, so to speak.) Chanting this prayer over and over is a powerful way to cleanse the body of guilt, shame, haunting memories, ill will, or bad feelings that keep the mind fixated on negative thoughts. As a forgiveness practice, it deeply resonates because it tends to penetrate our inner monologue over time. To try it out for yourself, and to "cleanse" yourself of bad feelings, chant the following mantra repeatedly while sitting with your eyes closed as a kind of meditation.

The Ho'oponopono prayer goes like this:

"I'm sorry. Please forgive me. Thank you. I love you."

That's it. And isn't that something we all need to hear? "I'm sorry. Please forgive me. Thank you. I love you." It's very touching, especially given how simple and universal these words are. With regular practice, reciting these four simple phrases helps develop self-love and self-esteem at the times when we need it most. In this way, it's both a lullaby to the self and a guaranteed insightful way to approach forgiving other people.

> *"Holding on to resentment is like taking poison and waiting for your enemies to die."*
>
> — Jen Sincero

EXERCISE

1. Who do you need to forgive besides yourself?

   _____
   _____
   _____

2. Which areas of your life need healing?

   _____
   _____
   _____
   _____
   _____

3. How do you act when no one is watching?

   _____
   _____

4. Go outside and walk and talk to yourself out loud for ten minutes. See what happens. Write down what came to you.

   _____
   _____
   _____
   _____
   _____

5. Practice the Ho'oponopono mantra with yourself. Write down how you feel afterward.

   _____
   _____
   _____
   _____

FIVE TIPS FOR HEALING YOUR LIFE

1. Read books and use their wisdom in your new life.

2. Practice forgiveness and let go of the past.

3. Heal your heart and love more.

4. Strengthen your mind and be kind to yourself.

5. Change how you see the world, and the world will change.

SUMMARY

Emotional healing is essential to living a great life of gratitude, to beautiful love relationships, to master your work, and to perform expertly. Becoming a more positive thinker will not make everything amazing. But with messy emotional and toxic feelings being carried from past harm, you will never deliver the creativity, productivity, performance, and peace you're looking for. With pain, anger, and sadness in your heart, you will never find the love of your life and keep them. You will never have long-term friendships or lifetime clients. The goal is to make your tragedy your triumph. The pain you healed will be the story you tell to help heal others.

I truly believe being successful in all areas comes down to healing your heart and healing from your past—that's when the magic will happen. When you heal your heart, your mind will automatically be more positive and your body can release stress, weight, and disease. Most importantly, you can truly connect to your soul and your life purpose. When you emotionally heal, you will be uplifted, your energy will be contagious, your charisma will attract others, and your energy will spread love.

"Life is an illusion created by your perception, and it can be changed the moment you choose to change it."

— Unknown

CALL TO ACTION

Call five people you must forgive. Start healing your life now.

Recognize patterns and pivot fast out of them. Say, "I love you" to yourself daily.

I encourage you to start using the Ho'oponopono mantra with yourself and others.

"One of the most courageous decisions you'll ever make is to finally let go of what is hurting your heart and soul."

— Brigitte Nicole

Chapter 10

Rocking the Boat

"On the level of courage, we are willing to take self-improvement courses, learn consciousness techniques, and risk the journey within to seek our own true Self, the inner reality. There is a willingness to experience uncertainty, periods of confusion, and temporary upset because, underneath the temporary discomfort, we have a long-term transcendent goal. The mind that is operating on the level of courage makes such statements as: 'I can handle it,' 'We'll make it,' 'The job will get done,' 'We can see this through,' 'All things shall pass.'."

— David R. Hawkins

Have you ever left your safe harbor to do hard things to grow? Is your life by your design? What would happen if you followed your heart? Are you ready to give up whatever is holding you back? Do you have the courage to jump into the unknown? In this chapter, I want to share a story of how I learned to rock the boat by following my heart; doing so had its risks, but in the end, it was worth it.

MY STORY

I was born and raised in Voorburg, a sub city of The Hague in the Netherlands. I studied in Amsterdam and most of my career was in The Hague, Amsterdam, Brussels, and Antwerp.

In October 2013, I met my wife Cheri in Amsterdam. She was visiting from the US to speak for Success Resources in the RAI in Amsterdam to 5,000 people who came to see Les Brown, Robert Kiyosaki, JT Foxx, Gerry Robert, and Cheri Tree. I bought Cheri's BANK system to increase my sales up to 300 percent and have more meaningful relationships.

I loved the training and became a certified licensed trainer. I built a very successful business selling and teaching the BANK system. Because of my success, Cheri came back to the Netherlands four months later to fulfill her Codebreaker Summit and Certify the European group. We traveled for thirty days through the Netherlands, UK, Sweden, Belgium, and France, and ended in Geneva, Switzerland, where we fell in love and had our first kiss on Valentine's Day.

We started a long-distance relationship between Antwerp and Las Vegas. We saw each other every six to eight weeks. In July, Cheri asked me to marry her, and I said, "Yes." In November 2014, I made the big jump over the pond. This was by far the hardest decision I have made in my lifetime. It was an emotional journey of letting go of my family, friends, home, business, career, and culture. I moved with three suitcases of clothes. I sold the rest or donated to people in need. I cried my eyes out the whole flight—eleven hours of snot and tissues. It was hard.

"I don't regret difficulties I experienced; I think they helped me to become the person I am today. I feel the way a warrior must feel after years of training; he doesn't remember the details of everything he learned, but he knows how to strike when the time is right."

— Paulo Coelho

At age thirty-nine, I arrived in the US. I spoke English, but far from great. I only knew Cheri. The adventure was fun and challenging at the same time since I didn't know anyone, didn't speak fluent English, faced ridicule, and had to deal with tough comments like, "You're only with Cheri for her money." When I met Cheri, she had just moved out of a storage unit where she had lived for eighteen months. I didn't date her for money. I have never dated anyone for their money. We moved in together in Scottsdale, Arizona, where the headquarters of Codebreaker Technologies was. I joined the team as vice president of sales and started traveling around the world with Cheri and speaking on stages.

In January 2015, we got married. No one knew we got married. We needed the legal papers to start the green card process. I have never felt more insulted and discriminated against in my life than when going through this process. I was treated by the immigration authorities like a criminal for almost two years. The questions, assumptions, and comments were outside my norm. Every time I went through customs in the US, they held me hostage for two hours to make sure I was not bringing in drugs or had other nefarious reasons to be here. Cheri had to wait with our luggage for hours, not knowing if they were going to send me back or I would walk through the door to go home.

After two years, I received my green card. During that time, I didn't see my family and friends in the Netherlands because I couldn't leave the country during my green card process. After five years, it got renewed for another ten years. Studying for the immigration test and taking the tests and interviews were among the hardest things I had to do. I had to memorize facts I'm sure most Americans don't even know. And we had to create a file with proof we were a couple and getting married for the right reasons. We had to document everything, from flight tickets and pictures to stories from our friends to testify it was real.

This was all reason enough to just go back home—but I didn't.

I didn't know what I had gotten myself into. Within three months, I realized one of Cheri's two business partners and friends was too big of a part of Cheri's life. I felt like I lived in a threesome. She was in our face every day, all day, all year in the business as well in our personal life. Wherever we went, there she was. She mastered inviting herself. She was just too much; I hadn't married her, and I didn't want her in my inner circle. She is a good person with a big heart, but it was just a very unhealthy situation. We untangled this in 2018, and it improved our relationship and life.

If this weren't enough reason to fly straight back to Amsterdam, my gut had been telling me from day one that Cheri's other business partner had the wrong intentions. He had hurt Cheri big time in 2008, and I had a premonition it would happen again. Cheri trusted him, but I didn't. I gave her an ultimatum: "It's him or me. I won't marry you if he is part of the business and your life." A few days later, we locked him out of all systems and bank accounts. Soon after, Cheri found out he had embezzled a million dollars and put her company in a tremendously difficult situation. We emotionally pivoted out of that quickly and financially recovered from it in the next months and years.

I felt I was going two steps backward for every one step forward. However, I knew the situation was temporary and would make me stronger and more resilient. I had to have faith and trust the process. Things happen for a reason. When you're in the midst of them, you don't know why until later.

The cultural differences I faced when I moved to the US were challenging. The first thing I noticed was how different humor is in the US compared to in Europe. In the European lifestyle, things aren't as serious as they are here in many cases. I had to learn the hard way when some of the things I said to people were taken the wrong way. The Dutch are known for their kindness but also their directness. Americans are very talented at sugar-coating messages. The Dutch and Europeans live a very balanced life where friends, family, outdoors, vacations, and five-hour meals with friends are normal.

The most ridiculous phrase I hear is at restaurants when the server says, "No rush. Take your time," after they just delivered your meal in ten minutes and put the bill on the table fifteen minutes later. You're literally in and out of a restaurant in thirty minutes. Time is money. So, when I sit down, the first thing I say is, "We are going to have dinner European style, and I will ask for the bill when we're ready."

I have never heard the phrase "going Dutch" more often than in the US. In the Netherlands, I rarely experienced that way of paying the bill. Also in the US, servers live on tips; in Europe, a tip is a nice extra but not required. The American lifestyle is different in many ways. You can make way more money here than in Europe. But money is not everything. That's why I preach about balance and creating a life with all forms of wealth, from health to quality time, from selfcare to friendships, from working hard to traveling more, from earning money to making a difference.

Food is a strange phenomenon here. You can find fast food restaurants everywhere. It's fascinating, even after living here for ten years. I often have Cheri go to these places without me or I stay in the car. The smell of fat is disgusting to my nose and tummy. European food is healthier and less processed than in the US. What is allowed here in food is not allowed in Europe. The poison they put in American food is bad and addictive. That's why people over twenty face obesity at a shocking rate of 71 percent. When I moved to America, I tasted sugar in everything I ate. To stay healthy and not gain weight, I really must watch what I eat. You can give me a Dutch herring any day over a processed hotdog.

In Europe, holidays seem to be more about the people, the connections, and the fun. The food and snacks are healthier, smaller plates, quality over quantity. In the Netherlands, we like to sing, dance, eat healthy, and drink. The Dutch know how to party. Two big party days in the Netherlands are Dutch Kings Day and Gay Pride. These days are fun. People are off work, street parties and music are everywhere, streets are decorated in orange, people wear orange, and strangers party together until late in the night. In Long Beach, California, they celebrate Dutch Kings Day. We go every year to dance, eat Dutch food like herring, *kroketten* (a deep-fried snack made of meat ragout covered in breadcrumbs), *ontbijtkoek* (breakfast cake), *poffertjes* (mini-pancakes), *stroopwafels* (waffles with a syrup in them), and Indonesian food. The local Dutch people come to hang out and proudly wear their orange. (Orange symbolizes our national pride; the Dutch royal family descends from William of Orange, who led the Dutch War of Independence against Spain in the sixteenth century.) You will never be able to take the Dutch out of me.

I know my destiny was to be here with Cheri to live my life, to fulfil my dreams, to help more people, to speak, to write, to share, and to bring Kai into our family. This has not been an easy ten years. They have simultaneously been my happiest and most challenging. I absolutely miss my friends, family, food, and culture.

And I love living in California for many reasons. The beautiful beaches, the hills, and the stunning landscapes. America has so many beautiful states, national parks, and different landscapes that will take your breath away. The customer service in general is exceptional, especially in the hospitality industry; Europe can learn from that. The USA has many advantages—anything is possible, no dream is too crazy to fulfill, and the money you can make here I would never make in Europe. That being said, I'm not money driven. I like a nice lifestyle, but more importantly, I'd love to impact lives and give back to humanity. When you have more money, you can give more. My entrepreneurial journey here expanded into opportunities I would never have back home in the Netherlands, like speaking on stage for thousands of people, and meeting Tony Robbins in person.

Will I ever move back to the Netherlands? No. If I move to Europe, it will be Italy, Spain, or Portugal.

"The universe has plans we don't know about; that's the beauty of life."
— Esther Wildenberg

LESSONS LEARNED

I learned life is a million steps, and we don't even know what the steps are until we face them. You can choose to take the step or not. The steps will always show up, and they will always be different. We will be shaken up, our path will keep changing, and our boat will be rocked. There will be no easy path, no straight line, or fairies. Magic mantras won't help. Only the action steps you take will move you into the next phase of your destiny.

When things went wrong in Cheri's and my relationship, I asked myself many times, "Why is this happening?" Connecting the dots backward, I know it happened to test our relationship and test whether our mission and vision would keep us going no matter what. We've passed both tests so far. We've met many more challenges in the past few years. We learned to pivot faster and better every time. Life is not an easy journey; it's our path to grow and learn new things.

And I expect many more to come. I'm ready for it.

One of my friends shared with me that to get better at something, to be the best, to achieve the success you have pride in, to make progress, is an uphill battle. You will have to hike up this hill, and there will be huge ditches, boulders rolling down, lakes of mud, and nasty weather. The list goes on. I believe that's true. I'm here to tell you growth is never linear. We constantly backslide and beat ourselves up for not living up to the expectations we create for ourselves. But when we can adopt the mindset of "One step forward, two steps back," I can guarantee you will see life through a lens of delicacy and compassion, not just toward others but more so toward yourself.

Every time I felt I moved back two steps, I took massive action to do one step forward. The biggest challenge is to get yourself going forward as fast as possible. It's all just one step of your lifelong journey of millions of steps. Sometimes we need steps backward to go forward in a different direction in relationships and business.

> *"The hardest thing to remember is that what we each really want is the truth of our lives, good or bad. Not rocking the boat is an illusion that can only be maintained by the unspoken agreement not to feel and in the long run it never really works. Let go of saving the boat and save the passengers instead."*
> — Kenny Loggins

EXERCISE

1. Name one difficult thing you can do.
   _____
   _____

2. Where do you feel you went two steps backward?
   _____
   _____
   _____
   _____

3. Come up with action steps to go one step forward.
   _____
   _____
   _____
   _____

4. Fly at 30,000 feet and write down the challenges you overcame.

_____
_____
_____
_____
_____
_____

5. Be a real friend and support someone you know whose boat is rocking right now. Write their name down and how you can help them.

_____
_____
_____

FIVE TIPS FOR ENJOYING EVERY STEP

1. Leave your safe harbor and explore what's out there.
2. Take two steps backward and see where the step forward takes you.
3. Ride the waves of life and enjoy it.
4. Know that a setback is not a long-term step backward.
5. See that the toughest times have made you stronger and more grateful.

SUMMARY

One step forward, two steps back. We use it to mean things aren't going smoothly. We use it to grimly express discouragement when it feels as if our efforts aren't yielding results, when our progress feels arduous. "Yup, one step forward, two steps back," we say. We use it to fake listen to others' challenges, like "Never mind; it will all work out," or "Everything happens for a reason." I hear you saying something about difficult times. "Yup, one step forward, two steps back." That substitutes for empathy. Like all good clichés, the phrase describes an actual, common experience. We've all found progress difficult at times, and it really is helpful to know others have experienced the same, but what might be more valuable than simply acknowledging the journey is recognizing why this happens.

> *"There is scarcely any passion without struggle."*
> — Albert Camus

Suppose you are renovating your bathroom. You have a plan, you have a budget, and it is going to be good. A weekend project, you declare. But when you pull out the toilet, it cracks. Now you must take the time and spend the money to get a new one. Boohoo. Things had been going so well. One step forward, two steps back.

You get the toilet sorted, but when you take the tub out, you find water damage and mold so you have to redo the walls and part of the floor. The weekend project becomes a full month of weekends, and the budget is now doubled. One step forward, two steps back.

Except no. The toilet was always going to crack—it was old and couldn't be moved. And the rot and mold were there behind the tub before you opened it up to see. It was always going to be a month-long, expensive project, and you were moving forward with it the entire time. The actual truth is you just wish it had been different.

> *"I never dreamed about success. I worked for it."*
> — Estée Lauder

This concept is harder to see when the movement has to do with personal growth. We have begun fitness routines many times, practiced faithfully for two or three months, and then become distracted by life and let it drop, leaving us back where we started. One step forward, two steps back.

Except no. You're not where you were. Not only have you put together two or three months of regular fitness, but you also now know something about getting started. Next, you need to figure out how to keep going. You were always going to struggle with maintaining the routine, a completely different skill from starting a new project. That's how this works. And when you get started again, you will be learning even more about how getting started works. You won't feel like some kind of renovation victim if you recognize the likelihood there will be additional surprises as part of the bathroom project. And you are far more likely to succeed in establishing a fitness routine if you respect that different stages are involved and you celebrate each new challenge as another step *forward* on your journey. And, of course, clichés are no substitute for actual empathy when talking to a friend.

So, maybe, we can put the phrase "One step forward, two steps back" to new use. When it is what we find ourselves wanting to say, we can look at where we need to pay closer attention.

Honestly, I thought it would be easy to move to the US, but my expectations became meditated resentments. Maybe I was a dreamer because I'm wired to the positive, the opportunity, and facing any challenge. I had to reset myself many times. I cried my eyes out a lot and had to get back up every time. It comes back to being honest with ourselves and loving ourselves through the process and the journey. It has not been easy, but anything worth fighting for isn't easy. It's called life.

> *"It's almost unbelievable where we are as a planet because people have been so afraid of rocking the boat, of putting forth what they really believe, and standing with people who need to be stood with."*
>
> — Alice Walker

CALL TO ACTION

Have faith when your boat is rocking. Jump into the unknown. I challenge you to save your friends and vision, not the boat. Build a new boat when it feels like the right decision. I encourage you to take a big step forward.

*"If you are always trying to be normal,
you will never know how amazing you can be."*

— Maya Angelou

Chapter 11

Life-Changing Routines

"Show me your routines, and I'll show you where you're headed."

— Mark Sephton

What routine has given you the greatest results? Who inspires you to have a routine? Why do you resist having a routine? Have you tried the 5 AM Club? What's your favorite habit and why? Let me share with you some life-changing routines I've developed for myself.

MY STORY

As a Capricorn, I'm a great organizer, but that doesn't mean it's my passion. I have always been more an action taker than a planner. In my mind, plans always change, so why plan in the first place? As I child, I had to follow routines and plans. I knew then that planning was not for me. And, of course, we must all go to school, go to practice, and join family gatherings. As a teenager, I pushed the boundaries of habit a lot. I decided when I should go home. I pushed the rules, not thinking of what I was doing to my mother's heart.

Most, if not all kids push the rules, boundaries, routines, and habits forced on them by parents and teachers. Kai is showing me that right now. He's a master at it. I guess I'm in payback time. And I love it.

I think I've always lived outside the box and wanted to create my life on my terms. I winged it a lot and loved it—until I read Robin Sharma's book *The 5AM Club: Own Your Morning. Elevate Your Life* in early 2019. This book changed my life for the better in so many ways. I didn't just read it; I used it in my life and business to the point that I joined his high-end mastermind group in 2022 to really connect with his philosophies and learn from him personally.

When I started to implement Robin Sharma's 5AM Club ideals, my days felt longer, more peaceful, less stressed, more productive, and much happier. I noticed the quiet time in the morning is peaceful and creativity flows. No one disturbs or distracts me at that time; most people sleep until it's time to get ready for work. The silence and solitude of the early morning energizes my soul, heart, body, and mind. It's like fuel pouring into a rocket ship. My days felt more organized, and I went to bed earlier, like 9 p.m. To be honest, nothing happens after nine, except TV or sometimes a party. I like a good party, so I will join these. I don't care about TV. Life is better with a morning routine, no doubt.

My demeanor at work changed. I started to plan my days and weeks differently and choose myself over any meeting, call, email, or text. I blocked my calendar for productive time in the morning and calls and meetings in the afternoon. I started to say no to most meeting invites and choose where I wanted to spend my time and energy to grow the business and focus on the things that made me feel fulfilled. I got so much more done, and by lunch time, I felt happy and accomplished, which fueled my jump into the afternoon.

I realized most meetings, email, and texts lead to more projects and more to dos, and that doesn't make me happy, so they went to the afternoon. Nothing can throw me off because I had my productive hours first. I don't look at email in the morning for a simple reason: I rarely receive an email where someone wants to write to thank or inspire me. Most of the time it's a question, request, problem, challenge, or project that needs my attention and time. I choose happy over busy.

When Kai was born in May 2020, my 5 AM Club got a new meaning. We were in the middle of the COVID lockdown and the club kept me sane, except that was now when Kai woke up and got his bottle and bath. Bye-bye, 5 AM Club routine for Esther. I had to adjust my routine to Kai's morning routine.

Babies master a routine from sleeping, crying, eating, and pooing—it's like clockwork, every two to three hours. I had to adjust when I could take care of myself. Most of the time it was when he fell asleep around 8 a.m. and before my first business meeting. It got harder after months of sleepless nights. I dropped my routine, and that undermined my happiness and inner peace. When Kai finally slept through the night at eighteen months, I slowly picked up my morning routine again. It made a huge difference.

As a mom, I realized how important routines are. From waking up to going to bed. From eating to changing diapers. From taking to school to playing. From giving a bath to reading stories. From giving him freedom to setting boundaries. Routines are great for everyone, and children will quickly teach us why. Routine is the difference between chaos and inner peace. Routines will change when your life changes. And following a routine that makes you happy makes a huge difference in how you feel and how your day goes. I highly recommend trying a morning routine for sixty-six days. It will change your life. It's like learning to ride a bicycle—it's hard the first two weeks; then it gets easier, and by the time you have done it for two months, it's a routine you will never unlearn.

"Accountability and hitting your goals have everything to do with you and your routines. You're on your own path; no one is here to save you."

— Esther Wildenberg

LESSONS LEARNED

The most important thing routines created for me is inner peace. By nature, I wouldn't think to create a plan, routine, habit, or structure. Over time, I realized when I build my train track first, aka create a routine and structure, my train can go way faster and face fewer obstructions. I had to learn to slow down to create a routine, daily habits, and clear goals. Doing so made my life so much easier and more productive. I get so much more done in a day and week. The best part is I don't just achieve my goals—I feel fulfilled.

The thing about routines is they don't require you to predict how you will feel in the future. Instead, they ask you to determine how you'll act despite how you might feel. That's powerful. Setting routines and habits is essential because they help you manage your time more efficiently. When you have a set routine, you know exactly what you need to do and when you need to do it. This helps you plan your day effectively and ensures you complete all your tasks on time. Routines and habits also help you stay focused and motivated. When you know what you need to do, you are less likely to get distracted by other things. You can focus all your energy on a task, which helps you complete it faster and with greater accuracy. Routines and habits can help you achieve your goals. When you have a set routine, you are more likely to stick to it.

The physiology behind building good habits is based on the concept of neural plasticity. Our human brain can change and adapt based on

LIFE-CHANGING ROUTINES

our experiences. When we repeatedly perform an action, our brain creates neural pathways that make it easier to perform that action in the future.

The psychology behind building good habits is based on the concept of willpower. Willpower is a finite resource—we have a limited supply of it each day. When we use our willpower to perform a task, we become mentally fatigued. However, when we perform a task repeatedly, it becomes a habit, and we no longer need to rely on willpower to perform it.

Several important daily habits and routines can help you unlock your full potential.

My *early* morning routine, starting at 5 a.m., starts with exercise, which is an essential daily habit that can help boost your physical and mental health. Then I meditate. Meditation is a powerful tool that can help reduce stress and anxiety and improve mental clarity.

Then I read and journal until 7 a.m. Reading is an excellent habit that can help improve your knowledge, vocabulary, and creativity. Journaling is a therapeutic habit that can help you process your thoughts and emotions.

At 7 a.m., I take Kai to school. Then I start my next routine.

My day routine, starting at 8 a.m., is a long walk on the beach to clear my mind and visualize my day and the outcome of my day.

I work on my projects and important goals for the first three hours. I don't take any calls, read email, or look at social media.

In the afternoon, I make/answer calls, check email, and respond to texts.

The last hour of my work day, I check my goals and plan the next day.

I meet my personal trainer, and the nanny picks Kai up from school.

My evening routine, before going to bed at 9 p.m., is to play with Kai and feed him his dinner. I give him a bath and read stories. Then Cheri takes Kai to bed.

Clean the home, pack Kai's backpack for the next day of school, and walk the dog.

Relax, read, and connect with Cheri. No digital devices. Go to bed at 9 p.m.

On the weekend, I plan my next week. Planning is an important routine that can help you manage your time more effectively and achieve your goals. I coordinate calendars with Cheri and plan trips, travel, and experiences.

Robin Sharma and Malcolm Gladwell inspired me to live with routines and habits. Gladwell defined the power of routine in his book *Outliers: The Story of Success*, studying the rise of Steve Jobs, Tiger Woods, the Beatles, and other phenomenal success stories. He determined through his research that to become a master at your craft, you must dedicate at least 10,000 hours to it. This is the minimum threshold of experience that will set you apart from amateurs and the rest of the world.

So many great examples of success stories based on strong routines and habits exist. Michael Phelps started swimming competitively at seven. By age ten, he already held a national record for his age group in the 100-meter butterfly. According to his coach, Bob Bowman, Phelps didn't miss a morning practice from age eleven to sixteen. He would practice on Sundays, birthdays, and Christmas mornings to keep his competitive edge. At an average of four hours per day in the pool, that meant Phelps had already shattered the 10,000-hour rule by the time he competed in his first Olympics in Sydney in 2000—the youngest male to make a US Olympic swim team in sixty-eight years.

LIFE-CHANGING ROUTINES

Elon Musk is one of the most interesting CEOs in the world. This South African tech mogul leads the way in the electric vehicle and renewables markets, and he's also behind Space X, the company promising to make space travel a reality, even for the average person. It would be fair to say he has some lofty goals set to a notoriously aggressive and optimistic schedule—referred to as "Elon time"—which often doesn't go to plan. However, he's a successful entrepreneur responsible for building some of the world's most innovative technology, rivaling Steve Jobs for the title of most innovative. Today, he splits his time between running his companies: Tesla, SpaceX, The Boring Company, and Neuralink. His day is organized into five-minute-long segments, and he often works so hard he skips meals. Musk is known to spend the night sleeping on the production floor or in a conference room just to eke out productivity gains. Elon Musk wakes up early, around 7 a.m., and gets things started with a shower. He often skips breakfast and prefers an omelet if he does eat breakfast. His work week is split between his various businesses. Most of his time is spent on design and engineering work. Musk prioritizes meetings and workflow, frequently cuts meetings short, and actively discourages unnecessary meetings. When he's not working, he likes to relax with some whiskey or wine, reading, and tweeting. He goes to bed around 1 a.m.

Tony Robbins, the world's most famous life and business coach, at sixty-five years old is busier than ever. He travels the world annually for about sixty events (which can last an hour or several days), goes on media tours for his latest projects, owns 107 companies, consults businesses and professional sports teams, and works with a small list of personal clients like billionaire investor Paul Tudor Jones. Robbins is a naturally energetic guy, but he's no longer twenty-five; to maintain the energy and productivity his schedule demands, he's developed a morning routine that packs a lot into a half hour. Around four years ago, Robbins hired Billy Beck III as his full-time personal trainer. Beck has had clients like Dwayne "The Rock" Johnson, NFL and NHL players, boxers, and UFC fighters. He's tailored nutritional and exercise programs for Robbins the same way he would for his athletes, customizing both for Robbins' metabolism and the physical demands of his seminars and lifestyle where time zones are rarely constant. Robbins wakes up between 7 and 9 a.m. after just three to five hours of sleep. After getting out of bed, he'll take a Beck-concocted "adrenal support cocktail" composed of a shake made of powdered greens, vitamin C, and antioxidants, along with capsules of methylated B vitamins mixed with additional nutrients. When he's done with his workout, he'll have a breakfast of free-range eggs and organic coconut bread. Robbins is far from a foodie and tends to stick with the same daily meals. Robbins created a ten-minute daily exercise called "priming," based on techniques found in yoga and Buddhist mindfulness meditation. One-minute breathing exercise, three minutes expressing gratitude, three minutes connection, and three minutes visualizing, followed by a fifteen-minute workout. Then his sixteen-hour workday starts. Although he works hard, his wife Sage, kids, and grandkids are his number-one priority.

I hope these stories inspire you to level up your own routines and start being more productive, reaching your goals, being happier, healthier, more fulfilled, and more grateful.

> *"You'll never change your life until you change something you do daily. The secret of your success is found in your daily routine."*
>
> — John C. Maxwell

EXERCISE

1. Take a pad of paper and write three column headings: personal, work, relationships.

_____

_____

_____

2. Under each heading write down everything you do during a typical week.

_____
_____
_____

3. Now, write down the things you would *like* to do in a typical week, for example:

   - Personal—read before bed each evening.

   - Work—read one interesting LinkedIn article; check in with an old colleague.

   - Relationships—go for a meal with friends.

_____
_____
_____
_____
_____
_____

4. What obstacles are likely to stop you from doing the things you want to achieve? Write down how you might reduce or remove those obstacles.

_____
_____
_____
_____
_____
_____

5. Find an accountability partner to do the routine with. Who would be your partner?

_____

_____

FIVE TIPS FOR CREATING ROUTINES

1. Start with easy routines but challenge yourself.
2. Write down what you really want in your life.
3. Set priorities in your life, relationship, and business.
4. Do more of what makes you happy.
5. Eliminate distractions and start planning your days.

SUMMARY

Life can be a whirlwind of decisions—what to eat, when to exercise, when to rest, when to connect with family and friends, and when to sneak in a few extra hours of work. How do we squeeze everything in? What if there were a way to simplify your day and boost your well-being at the same time? That is where establishing a routine can be your secret weapon. Establishing and maintaining daily routines can be a game changer because routines provide structure, promote consistency, and help embed healthy habits. Morning and evening routines are designed to support a healthier, more balanced lifestyle. Routines are a superpower for being happier, healthier, and wealthier.

Daily routines help establish and reinforce healthy habits by providing a consistent framework for daily activities. Over time, these habits become second nature. A routine can cut down on the depressing feeling of meeting day-to-day responsibilities. Routines create space for added brainpower by taking the guesswork out of daily tasks. You can focus on what matters, knowing you've got healthy habits in place. We all know the struggle of putting things off. Routines create a predictable schedule, making it easier to stick with your goals like exercise or meal prep. A routine feels empowering and organizes your day. It allows you to consistently make healthy choices, which boosts your confidence and motivation. Consistent sleep and wake times are key for good sleep. Routines help regulate your body's natural sleep-wake cycle, leading to better sleep and more energy throughout the day. Routines can reduce stress and anxiety by providing a sense of control and predictability. Knowing what to expect can make daily life feel more manageable and less overwhelming. A well-designed morning routine can set a positive tone for the day, boosting energy and productivity.

It is important to note that a routine is designed to create a predictable structure and assist with efficient decision making, but flexibility is a key component. Events can tilt your day or evening in one direction or another. You can find power in honoring the space you're in and moving forward intentionally. It's okay if routines need to be "tweaked" to accommodate shifts you and your family experience.

Find what works for you and personalize routines to fit your lifestyle and preferences. The key is to be consistent and find a rhythm that promotes healthy habits and makes you feel your best. So, ditch the daily scramble and embrace the power of routines. You might just be surprised at how much smoother and more fulfilling your life becomes.

Life is much happier and easier with daily routines, not just for you, but for your family, colleagues, activities, clients, travel, goals, and desires. Life will never be the same—just better when you start creating routines.

"It's okay if you fall and lose your spark. Just make sure when you get back up, you rise as the whole damn fire. Difficulty calls us to rise, and in that rising, we learn what we are capable of. Rise and shine. Your light is needed in the world. Rise and shine; it's a brand-new day to chase your dreams! Seize the day."

— Esther Wildenberg

CALL TO ACTION

I challenge you to try the 5 AM Club. Start new routines right away. Only when you decide and execute will you get different results. Have a morning, day, and evening routine. Inspire your friends and partner to do the same. I encourage you to consistently follow your new routine for at least sixty-six days.

"When you arise in the morning, think of what a precious privilege it is to be alive—to breathe, to think, to enjoy, to love."

— Marcus Aurelius

Chapter 12

Near-Death Experience

"I had to die to find my true self and life purpose."
— Esther Wildenberg

What does your heart tell you your true purpose is? Have you ever had a near-death experience? Are your guides talking to you in your dreams? Throughout life, have you ever felt you were on the outside looking in and not fitting in? Are you afraid of truly living? Are you connected to the Source—God? I've mentioned my near-death experiences a few times so far in this book. I'm sure you're curious about them. Now it's time for me to tell you that story.

MY STORY

I had the privilege of having two near-death experiences at the age of twenty-three when I was in the ICU after my accident. The ICU experience itself is worth writing a book about. It's just not my passion to write about the suffering and death of others. What I will share is my two totally different near-death experiences with the incredible messages they sent that changed my life forever. It was an extraordinary journey of soul connection.

I remember it like it was yesterday…. I was lying in bed in the ICU. It was late at night. It was quiet, just the machines making endless noise, beeps, tones, bells, and sometimes scary alarms. The alarms were more traumatic than being in the ICU. Suddenly, I felt an intense vibration and energy in my feet and legs. It got stronger, and I transformed into feeling nothing, like life was pushed out of me. I couldn't feel my feet or legs. Then the vibration went up to my hips, pelvis, and lower stomach. At that moment, I pushed the red button for the nurse. I asked her to call my girlfriend Mieke; it was urgent. The nurse told me it was almost 11 p.m. I had to wait until the next morning. I panicked and told her I felt life was being removed from me, and I needed her. For whatever reason, maybe her gut, the nurse decided to call my girlfriend. I don't remember my girlfriend's arrival.

I experienced a beautiful journey through a tunnel of white light. I was surrounded by white lights, white angels, white spirits, guides, and ancestors. I will never forget the feeling of being guided to the spirit realm. The light wrapped around me felt like the warmest embrace I have ever felt. It felt safe and familiar, like going home. The light around me was composed of angels with huge wings and huge smiles. I felt seen and like I belonged. They seemed to speak in an energetic telepathic language that felt like pure love and healing.

I compare the sound to that of dolphins. Still today, hearing and seeing dolphins brings me harmony and healing and connects me to nature's divinity and my soul's purpose. I have developed a relationship with the dolphins and can connect with them, manifesting them at any time here in Southern California.

Back to my near-death experience, I felt like I had entered a new environment with possibilities, excitement, eternity, and inner peace. The angels infused me with love and comfort.

I didn't want to go back to my human body, but the angels clearly said, "It's not your time yet. You've a big mission this lifetime; you have to go back."

When I opened my eyes, my girlfriend was next to me, holding my hand. I felt so much love and peace, knowing everything would be okay.

As I write, it has been twenty-six years since I had that beautiful experience. I came back with more love for life, my future, my girlfriend, my family, my friends, and all people.

"A near-death experience is an accelerator for transformation; it gives you a profound sense of purpose and a reminder that life is a precious gift."

— Esther Wildenberg

The next day, I had another near-death experience. This experience was totally different but as powerful as my first one. I left my body and was flying. When I looked down, I could see the nurses and doctors. I was floating in nothing but air and clouds. Suddenly, I saw mountains. I landed in a mountain meadow. It was very still, but I heard whispers. I saw a Native American tribal leader with a huge headpiece with white and brown feathers. He had a very charismatic and kind but intense face. He was sitting on a brown horse. He was surrounded by white horses and angels. Beaming white light came from the horses' manes. Their manes were flowing like a blizzard.

Suddenly, the sun was rising. The beautiful morning light came over us. The horses were dancing, and the Native American said, "It's time to be courageous."

He gave me a white and brown feather with a key attached to it and said, "It's time to let go of your childhood trauma and past. It's time to start living your divine life purpose. You're on a big mission this lifetime."

"What is my purpose?" I asked.

"You're here on earth right now to raise the vibration, speak your truth, and lead women and a few men to living their purpose and dreams, starting at a young age and not having to wait for some event to become who they are."

"How?"

"The *how* is not relevant," he replied. "You will find out how when the time is right. Remember the feather and the key; they will show up when you're on the right path at the right time."

Suddenly, the sky was filled with color. The air was warm and felt like a blanket of love, passion, power, and inner peace. He disappeared in the beautifully colored sky with the horses surrounding him. I tried to follow, but they vanished in a bright white light.

Moments later, I opened my eyes in my bed in the ICU surrounded by my mom, twin sister, younger sister, girlfriend, two nurses, and a doctor. I was happy and ready to heal, recover, and step into my long journey with determination and resilience.

> *"Don't wait for a near-death experience to start truly living. We're a heartbeat away from eternity, so seize the day in gratitude."*
>
> — Esther Wildenberg

LESSONS LEARNED

The spiritual world is beautiful, light, blissful, graceful, unconditional in its love, and perfectly peaceful. I have no doubt life is infinite and our human experience is to evolve our souls through the choices we make, the choices we don't make, the lessons we learn, the lessons we avoid, and the outcomes of these moments. When we come to earth, we're bright, light, loving, spiritually connected to Source, and faithful. We will be tested our whole life to see what we're made of.

We all experience challenges and events that leave marks, scars, and wounds on our soul. I believe we were created with the strength to ultimately heal our wounds and transmute our pain, suffering, and struggle into power. I've worked hard since I was twenty-three to find the truth of my soul journey. My life didn't get easier after having these experiences; they just gave me more hope and faith.

Life is a daily journey of lessons. Lessons are learned through blissful joy and extreme pain. Our pain can be our greatest teacher and blessing if we learn to embrace our endless lessons. Like my grandmother said, "You will learn every day, from your first breath until your last breath. I'm ninety and still learn every day." Instead of asking yourself, "Why did this happen to me?", lean in to see what the lesson is. Doing so will lead to your highest soul growth and soul purpose in this lifetime.

My biggest gifts were these two near-death experiences. The accident, hospital, rehab, and recovery time were not fun at all. But they taught me so much about my willpower, strength, determination, connection to the Divine Source, and unique talents and gifts.

In the human world, we experience separation, being divided and individualistic. We pray, hope, and dream. I felt we were all one. God is one, the Divine is one, all humans are connected as one. That's why every thought we have or action we take changes the whole.

The meaning of being on earth right now is to expand our souls and really feel self-love. We all want peace, love, and joy. We don't feel it if we don't love ourselves, aren't healing our hearts, and don't show our gratitude for all life experiences. Just like the ocean will always have waves, we will always experience waves in life. Waves of challenge and possibility. They ebb and flow. That's why I love my deep connection with the dolphins—they represent freedom, joy, going with the flow, spiritual connection, gratitude, and love.

The spirit world is asking us to see roadblocks as redirecting us to a better path. Rejection is God's protection. Our guides, spirits, ancestors, and angels guide us daily. It is the human path to feel that connection and trust its signs. We're here to raise our vibrations. The higher our vibration, the easier it is for spirits to reach us. We each can connect personally with our angels and loved ones in spirit. When a loved one transitions to the other side, we feel grief—one of the most painful lessons of life. Please understand death does not end the relationship; it changes relationships.

> *"We tend to take a great deal for granted, because you feel like you're going to live forever. It's only if you lose a friend, or maybe have a near-death experience, that many events and people in your life suddenly attain real significance."*
>
> — Brandon Lee

EXERCISE

Reflect on the questions below. Describe how you feel and what actions you can take.

1. What are the biggest lessons you learned so far in your lifetime?

_____
_____
_____

2. What humbling wakeup call have you had?

_____
_____

3. What's holding you back from living life to the fullest?
_____
_____
_____
_____

4. What is your life purpose and biggest dream?
_____
_____
_____
_____
_____
_____

5. Who is your example, and what do they reflect in you?
_____
_____

FIVE TIPS FOR LIVING LIFE TO THE FULLEST

1. Start seeing roadblocks as redirection.
2. Know life is not forever; start living now.
3. Expand your soul and love life.
4. Start listening to the signs of the Divine Source.
5. Learn to ride the waves; the ocean will always have them.

SUMMARY

Insights from near-death experiences (NDEs) are priceless and sometimes difficult to describe in the human world. Most people question what happens when we die. Thanks to my NDEs, I connected with spiritual teachings on a way deeper level. No worldwide religions will get you close to the experience of having an NDE. It's a unique experience that shapes you for the rest of your life.

> *"A near-death experience is a humbling reminder of our mortality and the fear of death fades away."*
>
> — Unknown

NDEs are profound experiences. They are a close encounter with death or a situation where death seemed imminent. These occurrences often transcend time, space, and our usual understanding of reality. Common NDE elements are experiencing a bright light, encounters with deceased relatives or spiritual figures, and feelings of indescribable love and interconnectedness. Many people who have had an NDE feel they've glimpsed the afterlife—a dimension far beyond the earthly plane. This fascination with the afterlife isn't mere esoteric indulgence. It's an exploration of our spiritual essence, and it plays a crucial role in our movement toward a more conscious way of living. In this grand quest, near-death experiences serve as lanterns—offering glimpses of what might lie beyond our mortal selves.

I've talked to many people who have had NDEs. Every NDE is unique, but certain elements appear with remarkable consistency across cultures, religions, and personal backgrounds. They often include:

- **A Sense of Leaving the Body:** People, whether in the operating room or at the scene of a grisly accident, commonly report feeling they were hovering over their physical forms, often witnessing others' attempts to revive them. In these moments, they can see and hear what is happening from a bird's eye view, yet their presence appears to go unnoticed. This happened in both of my experiences.

- **The Tunnel and the Light:** A tunnel or a pathway often appears during the person's NDE. At the end of this tunnel or pathway is a brilliant, loving, ethereal light that seems to beckon them forward. This only happened in one of my experiences.

- **Beings of Light:** Many of those who have this experience describe meeting loving entities. These entities may be relatives who have gone to the other side or angel-like or other divine beings. I experienced this in both NDEs.

- **Life Review:** An instantaneous review of a person's life (sometimes known as a "life reel") may occur, often accompanied by a profound sense of understanding and acceptance. It is as if one suddenly understands everything happened precisely at the right moment for optimal growth and spiritual development. I experienced this in one of my NDEs.

- **A Choice to Stay or Return:** Frequently, people report they were given a choice to return to their earthly existence or continue into the light. Some later explain why this was or was not an easy decision to make. I experienced this in both NDEs.

These elements of near-death experiences put together often bring an overwhelming sense of unity and oneness with the universe, a sentiment that echoes the core beliefs of conscious living.

I find it fascinating that an event so closely associated with death can teach us so much about the profundity and interconnectedness of life. One thing I learned through these experiences is I have a strong connection to the universe, God, guides, angels, ancestors, and spirituality. NDEs are transformative, paradigm shifting, creating a more conscious way of living and awareness of how short life is. They're extraordinary!

The journey toward understanding the afterlife and NDEs is not separate from our path to living consciously—a path where we make intentional decisions that align with our values and purpose. They are interwoven threads in the same cosmic tapestry. Just imagine what could happen when we reach that tipping point where roughly 10 percent of the global population embraces conscious living! We would ignite an unprecedented wave of positive change, harmonizing our existence in a manner we've only dared to dream of.

By going to retreats, meditating daily, and enjoying silence, solitude, and stillness, you can create a paradigm shift that can lead you as part of humanity into an era of unprecedented peace, love, and understanding with less judgment, more compassion, faith, kindness, joy, and seizing the day in love and gratitude.

> *"I never felt loved like I felt the love on the other side. I believe I took that love with me back to earth, to love life and love more deeply, and to show more love to everyone and live my life purpose."*
>
> — Esther Wildenberg

CALL TO ACTION

Accept that pain is our greatest teacher. I encourage you to read about being a spiritual being having a human experience. Embrace mortality's reality; no one knows their expiration date. I challenge you to raise your vibration. Do not wait for a life-changing event to truly be you.

"I believe love is why we're here on the planet and that ultimately, it's our purpose for life. They say people who've had near-death experiences often report back that at the end of our lives we have a life review, and we're asked one question, and that question is, how much did you love?"

— Marci Shimoff

Chapter 13

Let Go. Forgive. Surrender.

"If you want to fly in the sky, you need to leave the earth. If you want to move forward, you need to let go of the past that drags you down."

— Amit Ray

What am I grateful for? Do you feel something is dragging you down? Can you think of what is not serving you? Have you ever surrendered? What is the worst that can happen when you let go? Have you felt the power of letting go? Letting go is not easy so I'll share with you next a story of how I did it so you can learn how powerful it can be.

MY STORY

We have all experienced painful situations where we must let go of people or things we care about. I have been hurt many times, betrayed, cheated on, taken advantage of, manipulated, and used.

And I have done the same to others and even worse to myself. I'm no angel from heaven who lives in the light all the time, who is always happy, kind, and loving. Like every other human, I have made many mistakes and hurt people. I didn't hurt anyone intentionally; it happened because I didn't let go of my beliefs, my programming, and my experiences. In *The Body Keeps the Score: Brain, Mind, and Body in the Healing of Trauma*, Bessel van der Kolk, MD, talks about that in detail. I had to let go of many people I truly loved and wished were still in my life on a deeper level. Letting go of things is easy—I have no attachment to stuff. I like nice things, but great experiences are more important to me.

My first letting go experience was with my first boyfriend, whom I had to let go of and forgive. I was really in love for the first time. When he cheated on me with another girl who was older than me, we broke up. You may think, *No big deal*; after all, I was just thirteen, but it was my first heartbreak. He gave me a necklace with the first letter of his name on it, and I had to give it back. Looking back, it's kind of funny, but at thirteen, it was heartbreaking. Many boyfriends and girlfriends followed. My mom can tell you many stories.

We can all relate to heartbreak, going through separation, divorce, or ending any relationship. I'm still in touch with several ex-partners. I'm an all-in kind of person; I still love them because they all played an important role in my life, making me who I am today. I had to forgive and let go of what I thought we had many times. Letting go isn't easy; it's like training a muscle that never gets stronger.

> *"People get so in the habit of worry that if you save them from drowning and put them on a bank to dry in the sun with hot chocolate and muffins they wonder whether they are catching a cold."*
>
> — John Jay Chapman

Letting go of a job I really liked or a boss I truly admired has also been hard for me. I'm a very hard worker, and I pour my heart and soul into things I do. Pause for a moment and think about how much time you spend at your job or in your business. Vera was one of my favorite people I ever worked for. She was an amazing business owner and

CEO. She inspired me to get better every day. She had high standards and gave me a lot of responsibility.

When I asked Vera to mentor me, she did. She took me with her to business lunches, executive meetings, and client visits. When she sold the company and left, I had a hard time letting go. I felt appreciated, seen, heard, and recognized, but without her, I was not happy anymore at the company. I had to let go of the picture I painted; I had to forgive her for leaving and surrender to the new possibilities ahead of me.

One of my coaches once asked me, "How heavy is this glass of water I'm holding?" I thought she was going to ask if it was half-empty or half-full. I didn't answer and stared at her with big eyes, wondering what water glasses had to do with my healing and letting go, forgiving, and surrendering. She looked me straight in the eyes and said:

> From my perspective, the absolute weight of this glass doesn't matter. It all depends on how long I hold it. If I hold it for a minute or two, it's light. If I hold it for an hour straight, its weight might make my arm ache a little. If I hold it for a day, my arm will likely cramp up and feel completely numb and paralyzed, forcing me to drop the glass. In each case, the weight of the glass doesn't change, but the longer I hold it, the heavier it feels. Your sadness, anger, and worry are very much like the glass of water. Think about them for a while and nothing happens. Think about them a bit longer and you begin to ache a little. Think about them all day long, and you will feel completely numb and paralyzed—incapable of doing anything else until you drop them.

Sometimes I forget this metaphor and get hung up on my hurt feelings. It's important to remember to let go of sadness, anger, stress, and worry. No matter what happens during the day, as early in the evening as you can, put all your burdens down. Don't carry them through the night and into the next day. If you still feel the weight of yesterday's emotions, it's a sign it's time to put the glass down.

> *"Most people are stuck in the past; that's why they will never be happy."*
>
> — Esther Wildenberg

LESSONS LEARNED

Letting go is very powerful. Letting go means releasing all that does not serve us and releasing things we do not have control over from our focused attention. When we do, we free up so much space for fresh perspectives, creative ideas, and connection to the present moment, our loved ones, and ourselves.

When you let go of people who inhibit your inner peace or life purpose, you open the door for the next level of opportunities to enter your life. I've noticed things go much more smoothly when I give up control, when I allow them to happen instead of making them happen.

Like most humans, in the past I spent a lot of time in others' business—my child's, my friends', Mother Nature's, my family's. Meaning I tried to help them by preventing things from happening, giving them advice, and supporting them when they didn't ask for or want my help. Everyone is on their own life path, and we can't take away their learning experiences, including our own.

> *"You must learn to let go. Release the stress. You were never in control anyway."*
>
> — Steve Maraboli

We try to control things because of what we think will happen if we don't.

In other words, control is rooted in fear. Control is a result of being attached to a specific outcome—an outcome we're sure is best for us, as if we always know what's best.

When we trust we will be okay no matter what comes our way, we don't need to micromanage the universe. We let go. And we open ourselves to all sorts of wonderful possibilities that aren't there when we're attached to one "right" path. The energy of surrender accomplishes much more than the energy of control.

I suspect it's slightly different for everyone, but here's what control mode looks and feels like to me: My vision gets very narrow and focused, my breath is shallow, adrenaline is pumping, and my heartrate increases. My mind shifts from topic to topic and from past to future very quickly, and I have little concentration, poor memory, and almost no present-moment awareness. In surrender mode, I'm calm, peaceful, breathing deeply, and present in the moment. I see clearly and my vision extends out around me, allowing me to (literally) see the bigger picture. So, the great irony is that trying to control everything can actually make you feel less in control. When I'm micromanaging and obsessing over details, I know I'm in my own way.

Surrender means to stop fighting. Stop fighting with yourself. Stop fighting the universe and the natural flow of things. Stop resisting and pushing against reality.

Surrender equals complete acceptance of what is plus faith that all is well, even without our input. It's not about inaction. It's about acting from surrender energy.

If letting go of control and surrendering not only feel better but produce better results, how do we do that? Sometimes it's as easy as noticing we're in control mode and choosing to let go—consciously and deliberately shifting into surrender energy.

For example, when I see I'm in control mode, I imagine I'm in a small boat paddling upstream, against the current. It's hard. It's a fight. That's what control mode feels like to me. When I choose to let go and surrender, I visualize the boat turning around, dropping the oars, and floating downstream. I'm being gently pulled, no effort necessary on my part. Simply breathing and saying, "Let go of the oars," is usually enough to get me there. Sometimes it's a little harder to make the shift from control to surrender.

When you pinpoint the fear, question its validity. Ask yourself if it's true. If you're afraid the night will be ruined if your partner doesn't remember to pick up eggplant (and you've already reminded them fourteen times), question that assumption. Can you really know the night would be ruined without the eggplant? And if it would (by your definition, anyway), what's so bad about that? Your business is the realm of things you can directly influence. Are you there? Or are you in someone else's business? When we're trying to control things outside of our own business, it doesn't go well.

Let the feeling of freedom guide you toward loosening your grip.

Einstein said, "The most important decision we make is whether we believe we live in a friendly or hostile universe." I believe in a friendly universe. Being receptive and allowing things to happen is a skill we can practice and improve. It helps to believe in a friendly universe—one that supports you at every turn so you don't have to worry over the details. We can always choose to do things the easy way. We can muscle through, or we can let go of the oars and let the current carry us with the flow. A peaceful, yet focused energy accompanies holding the intention of what I want but not forcing myself to do it. That energy is magic. I'm still a work in progress, but I'm allowing it to become a habit instead of making it a habit.

LET GO. FORGIVE. SURRENDER.

"To let go does not mean to get rid of. To let go means to let be. When we let be with compassion, things come and go on their own."

— Jack Kornfield

EXERCISE

1. What or who will you let go of today?

_____
_____
_____

2. What or who are you grateful for? Write down ten things.

_____
_____
_____
_____
_____
_____
_____
_____
_____
_____

3. Where are you winning and making progress?

_____
_____
_____
_____
_____

4. Who is bothering you and why? It may be time to let in love and light.

_____
_____
_____
_____

5. Do you recognize any similarities between people and circumstances?

_____
_____
_____
_____

FIVE TIPS FOR LETTING GO

1. Surround yourself with people who love you unconditionally.

2. Rejection is God protecting you—believe it; it happens 100 percent of the time.

3. Protect your energy and time. See where it flows clearly.

4. Write in your journal and love yourself in the process.

5. Let them be. They're on their own path. Not your journey.

SUMMARY

Letting go is one of the most profound lessons I ever learned, and it helped me to quickly get through betrayal and pain. Read this carefully. The kabbalists, Jewish mystics who study and practice Kabbalah, teach we come into this world to do the spiritual work of transformation so we can earn that *Light*. Therefore, when we're giving something to a person or doing something for them they have not earned, we are giving them the *Bread of Shame* because they are receiving fulfillment without effort; they are not doing the work of transformation they need to do to earn the *Light*.

We are here, of course, to help others and share with them. But we do that differently depending on the person's level of consciousness. The Kabbalah teaches that to truly help someone they must desire change. If they don't want to make the effort, trying to help them anyway is called the Bread of Shame. Your act of transformational sharing in such a situation might, therefore, be to give the person the space to earn the Light themselves. For many of us, this is difficult. When we see someone hurting or struggling, we want to help them. However, they must do it themselves. This is, in fact, not only the most loving and sharing thing we can do for them, but also an act of transformational sharing, because we go beyond our own comfort zone.

The more uncomfortable the sharing is for us, the more light it reveals, and the greater the transformative power of those actions—both for our own lives and the lives of those we have shared with.

> *"The more anger toward the past you carry in your heart, the less capable you are of loving in the present."*
>
> — Barbara De Angelis

We must defend ourselves against all the negative information out there through the regular practice of deliberately recognizing our blessings, no matter how small.

To fuel momentum and protect your positive energy, it's mission-essential to constantly celebrate progress. Noting your micro-wins in your notebook is a splendid way to battle-proof hope and bulletproof inspiration so that you stay on course when hard influences push you off.

Harboring resentment toward those who have wronged you is to carry them on your back.

Forgiveness isn't condoning bad behavior. It's simply understanding everyone does the best they can based on their level of consciousness. (Even if their best is a mess.)

Journaling about painful feelings allows you some emotional healing and a way to release resentment so you don't carry the baggage into your brighter future. Journaling just a few lines on what a strong and wise day looks like will lock your focus into what's most important instead of keeping busy being busy. Forgiveness can keep you from climbing mountains that, at the end of the year, turn out to be the wrong ones.

Journaling and writing is healing.

Write a quick paragraph reminding yourself what you want to be said about you, your character, your accomplishments, and your kindness, when your fine life is over. This ritual trains your brain to help you live to the point. So, when you arrive at the end, you will have concentrated on the right priorities and lived your life well.

I created a new morning routine that helped me stay grounded and connected to my truth, my heart, my mission, and my path this lifetime:

- Journal—write down the ten things I'm grateful for.
- Send Love—send love to the three people who bother you right now.
- Be Quiet—meditate for five minutes (or longer).
- Say the Ho'oponopono Prayer—repeat seven times to yourself (or think of others): "I'm sorry. Please forgive me. Thank you. I love you."
- Ask—ask for guidance for the day.

LET GO. FORGIVE. SURRENDER.

"Life is really simple, but we insist on making it complicated."

— Confucius

CALL TO ACTION

I encourage you to learn to let go faster every time you get hurt. The faster you can forgive, the faster you can pivot away from the emotion. Logic comes back more quickly, and you rise above the situation. Be honest with yourself by seeing where you betrayed yourself by not listening to your gut instinct and created the situation subconsciously so you could grow. Start journaling before you go to bed and when you wake every day.

Chapter 14

Find Your Tribe

"Never doubt that a small group of thoughtful, concerned citizens can change the world. Indeed, it is the only thing that ever has."

— Margaret Mead

Who inspires you? Who teaches you? Who can you teach? Who is open to learning from you? Who brings you joy? Who understands you? Who holds you accountable? The answers to those questions are the people who make up your tribe. In this chapter, I'll share how I found my tribe and how you can find yours.

MY STORY

I've been thinking recently about the incredible people I've been fortunate to surround myself with during my twenty-five-year career and fifty years on this planet. They've all played key roles in my career and life. They've been there for the good, the bad, and everything in between. Some were there for a reason and a season but not a lifetime.

My tribe has changed many times over the years. According to the dictionary, a tribe is a group of people who are united by shared cultural, religious, or social values. I'd like to expand that definition to include presence, interest, passion, personality, EQ (emotional quotient), SQ (spiritual quotient), and vibration (energy).

A tribe is home, a group of people where you can be 100 percent yourself without judgment. When I evolved and developed personally, my tribe changed.

As a child, my extended family were my tribe. I would say my sisters and cousins were my tribe. We spent many weekends together, playing soccer, riding bikes, building forts, walking the dogs in the woods, picking blueberries, playing games, doing naughty things, and creating trouble. I felt the most connected to my cousins. I didn't have many friends in school. Being identical twins wasn't easy for my sister and me, or for our classmates or teachers. I didn't belong to any friend group or kid tribe.

When I started playing field hockey, my team, club, and hockey community became my tribe. I saw them three times a week. I loved winning and playing the game. The third half, the party afterward, was always fun. As a team we had many tournaments, events, and parties. We were a cool tribe. Sports are a great way to become part of a tribe. When you share the same interest, you automatically connect on a deeper level. One of my best friends played field hockey with me thirty-five years ago; she's still my friend and part of my inner tribe. I lost most of my tribe when I had my accident at twenty-three. I couldn't play field hockey anymore, so I became an outsider. I still love the game, and I cheer for the Dutch team every time they play.

I didn't really have a tribe at the university. I went to the university for dentistry. It was not my passion in the first place, just a great occupation where you could make good money. I didn't like the profession, but I still finished my studies and started working in the industry. When you are pushed into a tribe, it's never really your tribe. When it's your choice by passion or interest, you find your people. I had maybe two good friends at the university, so it wasn't my most glorious time. Even in my work environment, I didn't really click with my colleagues. They loved what we did, and I hated it. I was still known as a great professional, and my patients loved me. My patients were my tribe.

During rehab after my accident, I had no tribe for a long time until I was able to join a gym and fitness center. I hired a personal trainer and went almost every day. I saw the same people, and we started to talk about exercise, the body, healing, health, and the commitment it takes to be in shape and in great condition. Working out with friends made it so much easier. They supported me, kept me accountable, and cheered me on in becoming an instructor. Spinning became my new passion. I joined the class a few times a week and then became a spin instructor, teaching classes four times a week. Having a spinning tribe was great. Exercise, sports, and a club are such a wonderful way to find your tribe. When you move together, energy blends beautifully and great friendships are born.

My career is very diverse. My resume doesn't make any sense, so my work tribe changed many times, although the people I was attracted to stayed the same—I had my people. We had the same values, similar personalities, great presence, and drive to succeed. We had big goals, got better every day, and were even a little competitive. I worked mostly with men; I would say 95 percent of my work tribe were men. I fit in well with a masculine vibe and can keep up with men's jokes, so working with them was easy. Men are simple creatures; women are way more complex and dramatic. Working with men was enjoyable. I was not a target for their hunting. They all knew I had a girlfriend and they couldn't "fix me." My careers in finance, human resources, information technology, security, government, fitness, and health gave me a great opportunity to see a lot of different industries, cultures, and tribes.

I knew corporate wasn't my fulltime, forever tribe. As a consultant for Fortune 500 companies, I thrived because I could bring my expertise and experience but not be in it five days a week. The older I get, the more I realize I fit in easily with many tribes. I connect fast with people wherever I go. Yet I still have my preference as to where I spend my time and with whom.

When I started my own business in 2008, I had to build my own tribe. As a freelancer, consultant, retreat host, mastermind group facilitator, speaker, and executive coach, my client base changes all the time. My tribe was mostly other consultants, freelancers, and coaches. We shared our passion for being our own boss, the freedom of time and money, and sharing wisdom with each other. We collaborated a lot, and I enjoyed being an entrepreneur and business owner. I joined several groups and networking communities. It was a totally different experience.

My tribe changed again when I moved to the United States in 2014. I left behind everything I had built in my home country over thirty-nine years to start from scratch. Change is not always easy. It was hard in the beginning, but soon I became part of my partner's company community. Over the past decade, I have found several tribes—most of them are successful entrepreneurs, business owners, world travelers, mastermind and retreat lovers, and people who live life to the fullest. Life is short, so I know how important it is for my happiness, success, and legacy to be part of the right tribe.

> "Find your tribe. You know, the ones who make you feel the most you. The ones who lift you up and help you remember who you really are. The ones who, when you walk out of a room, make you feel like a better person than when you walked in. They are the ones who, even if you don't see them face to face as often as you'd like, you see heart to heart. That is your tribe."
>
> — Esther Wildenberg

LESSONS LEARNED

Finding your professional tribe is crucial to your success. That may seem obvious, but as a student and young professional, I didn't know how to find my tribe, community, mentors, and business friends. No one explained how critical it would be to build a network to support you. I learned quickly who you know is more important than what you know.

You will thrive when you are part of a supportive and like-minded community. It doesn't matter if you are just starting out or a seasoned professional—the importance of discovering and nurturing your professional tribe cannot be overstated. I learned that twenty-five years ago, and because I have always made it a priority, it has served me well.

Building a professional tribe is not just about finding like-minded people to network with; it's about fostering a supportive community aligned with your values and goals, while exposing yourself to unique viewpoints based on different experiences. The right tribe offers significant benefits. It's collaborative initiative.

> *"I define connection as the energy that exists between people when they feel seen, heard, and valued; when they can give and receive without judgment; and when they derive sustenance and strength from the relationship."*
>
> — Brené Brown

Your professional tribe includes people who share your dreams, values, and goals. Being part of this group means joining others who understand you and offer unwavering support and shared unity. Within your professional tribe, members bring diverse skills and expertise. Engaging with this group lets you tap into a wealth of knowledge and experience, helping you learn faster. The collaborative atmosphere encourages ongoing growth and keeps you updated with industry trends and best practices. You learn together and you grow together.

Finding your tribe is all about building strong connections that last. Networking is crucial for career success, and your tribe enhances these efforts. The connections you build within your tribe open doors to new opportunities, partnerships, and collaborations. As you connect with other focused people, your professional circle expands, increasing the odds of finding valuable contacts.

The professional journey is filled with ups and downs. Your tribe provides emotional support during tough times. Tribe members offer encouragement, empathy, and advice to help you navigate difficult situations. They are your emotional support system.

Being in a tribe pushes you out of your comfort zone. The trust and encouragement from the group increase your confidence, motivating you to take risks and pursue opportunities you might hesitate to explore otherwise. The right tribe will boost your growth and confidence. Tribes foster innovation and creativity. Collaborative idea-sharing sessions lead to groundbreaking solutions and concepts that might not emerge on your own. Diverse perspectives within your tribe spark fresh ideas, creating an innovative culture.

Surrounded by motivated professionals, you're more likely to stay committed to your goals. Tribe members act as a motivating force, encouraging you to strive for excellence and stay on track. They motivate you and keep you accountable. It's not just about what you gain from these relationships; it's also about what you give. A strong tribe relies on each member's dedication and care for one another. Just as much as you need support, others do too—and it feels amazing to help people you care about when they need you. It's mutual support.

In a world that celebrates individualism and separation, immense power exists in finding your professional tribe. Be the one who starts a tribe, a movement. I believe anyone could start a movement. Finding your tribe may be the hardest thing you do because you're probably looking in the wrong places or because they are already right in front of you. You are the sum of all the people you have ever met; you change the tribe, and the tribe changes you. Be the change you wish to see in the world.

"A tribe is a group of people connected to one another, connected to a leader, and connected to an idea. For millions of years, human beings have been part of one tribe or another. A group needs only two things to be a tribe: a shared interest and a way to communicate."

— Seth Godin

EXERCISE

Reflect on the questions below. Describe how you feel and what actions you can take.

1. Who lifts you up the most?

_____
_____
_____

2. What is your biggest interest in joining a tribe?

_____
_____

3. When do you judge people, and when do you feel judged?

_____
_____
_____
_____

4. Are you currently part of a tribe? What do you love about it?

_____
_____
_____
_____

5. What values, personality, and presence does your ideal tribe have?

_____
_____
_____
_____
_____
_____

FIVE TIPS FOR FINDING YOUR TRIBE

1. Join a tribe with shared interest and values.
2. Follow your passion and you will attract your tribe.
3. Be the leader who starts a tribe based on your passion, values, and interest.
4. Know when you feel heard, seen, and loved that you have found your tribe.
5. Reach out to a like-minded person when you feel lonely—remember, you're not alone.

SUMMARY

We all want to belong and be part of a tribe of some sort. A tribe or community is essential for well-being. We are wired for connection, and deep, meaningful relationships are crucial for emotional, mental, and spiritual well-being and fulfilment.

Being part of a tribe or starting a community requires authentic relationships, which require vulnerability. To build real connections, you must be willing to be vulnerable. Sharing your true self, including your struggles and fears, fosters trust and deepens relationships. Sharing is not always easy, but when you get comfortable with it, a new world will open for you and real friendships will be born. Community doesn't happen by accident. You need to be intentional about seeking relationships, making time for others, and prioritizing connection. You must be intentional with your effort.

Despite being more connected than ever through technology, many people feel lonely. It's important to look for and invest in face-to-face relationships. Loneliness is a modern epidemic. Most people wait for others to reach out or initiate deeper conversations. I encourage you to take the first step, whether it's inviting someone over, sharing your story, or expressing care. Be willing to take the first step; it will pay off. You can create a welcoming environment where people feel they can be themselves without judgment. Such an environment is vital for fostering genuine connections. Relationships aren't always easy or perfect. Embracing the messiness, including misunderstandings and conflicts, is part of building strong, lasting connections. In any community, people will hurt each other, intentionally or unintentionally. Practicing forgiveness and extending grace helps maintain and deepen relationships. When you're authentic and real, people will feel your heart and intentions. Remember, friends say what you want to hear; real friends tell you what you need to hear.

Consistent interactions are the backbone of deep relationships. Whether it's weekly gatherings, regular check-ins, or shared activities, consistency builds trust and familiarity. You must make your tribe a priority, even if it's just via text message.

And while it's good to be friendly with many, I recommend focusing your energy and investing in a few deep, meaningful relationships. These close connections will provide the support, encouragement, and accountability we all need. Remember, the five people you hang out with most are who you become. Create your own tribe or join one where you can be 100 percent you.

> *"Great leaders don't water down their message in order to make the tribe a bit bigger. Instead, they realize that a motivated, connected tribe in the midst of a movement is far more powerful than a larger group could ever be."*
>
> — Seth Godin

CALL TO ACTION

Use your digital devices less. Focus more on face-to-face relationships.

I challenge you to connect weekly with people you really care about. Connect deeper with people; talk about real things. Join a tribe, a community. Love people.

"Some people will hear you louder in silence. Those are your tribe—they'll get you through the tough days and give you something to laugh about on the ride."

— Nikki Rowe

Chapter 15

Don't Die

"The soul drives us to grow, achieve, search, learn—all in a singular quest to become more. Whether a business or a human, if we squelch this life force, the process of dying ensues. We are either growing or dying; the choice is ours."

— Unknown

Are you in the habit of investing in self-growth? Do you feed your soul? Do you read books? Do you surround yourself with people who have what you want? Do you like who you are? If we stagnate, we might as well be dead. I now want to share with you how I stay alive and well by continuing to focus on my growth.

MY STORY

I am often reminded, "You're either growing or dying." Businesses, like people, are living organisms, and they either grow or die. About twenty-seven years ago, I had a choice: suffer and be a victim, saying, "This accident happened to me," or fight for my life and create a new and better future. My two near-death experiences gave me so much clarity, showing me why I was here on this planet; I had no other choice but to become the person I had to be to live up to my potentional and purpose. It was a long journey, and I'm still on it. There's always another experience to help me grow, expand into the next level, serve more people, and grow my legacy.

I credit my dysfunctional childhood and difficult relationship with my parents with shaping me into the compassionate and insightful person I am today.

Sometimes, I took major leaps forward and ended up in a situation completely outside my comfort zone. That forced me to rise to another level, to grow and adapt to a new situation. Early in my career, someone else usually set those targets or challenges for me. They saw my potential before I did and wanted to give me the opportunity to grow faster.

Being pushed and having enough support was a personal growth point, and it slowly became my new normal and comfort zone. Sometimes these growth stories were visible to everyone around me. I was praised along the way and applauded at the end. I had that experience, literally, when I did my first speech at my corporate job.

Other times, my growth happened quietly, with baby steps, with no one noticing. I might not even have noticed it myself. Over two decades, I've read dozens of personal development books and attended dozens of events, courses, webinars, and more. The skills and habits I embodied were small, daily routines and directing my thoughts. Step by step, over time, they built my character and helped me grow.

I learned how valuable taking time off from everything is. It gave me time to stop, reflect, and let my subconscious take in all I had learned over the weeks, months, and years. I focused on the now, on how to clear my mind simply with controlled breathing and meditation. That's also growth. It's giving myself the time and space for my mind to do its job. These are all points of growth in the right direction, but they are not yet fine-tuned enough to my liking. I still have so many more opportunities to grow—they will never stop.

> *"The nature of life is to grow."*
>
> — Maharishi Mahesh Yogi

I spent most of my young adult life waiting for someone to tell me what to do next. Guess what? After thirty years of rotating around the sun, I started to listen to myself, my soul, my heart, and my mind. And now, after fifty trips around the sun, I believe the only place to find the answer is within.

I am not saying I came equipped with the answers to my most burning questions within myself. I am merely suggesting I will know the right answer when it comes to me. My job is to remain open, to search, and most importantly, to listen—to listen to myself, to those who inspire me, and even to those I do not trust. Throughout my daily life, I am granted many opportunities to see things differently or to consider new perspectives.

> *"I don't regret difficulties I experienced; they helped me become the person I am today. It's not about remembering the details but knowing how to strike when the time is right."*
>
> — Esther Wildenberg

LESSONS LEARNED

Whether learning a new language, trying a new activity, or even attempting a new challenge, making growth a priority—and a habit—will make your life one of dynamic improvement. Whether in business, personal relationships, or daily life, we are either growing or dying. The choice is ours. This choice is important because when we commit to searching for answers and growth, we are no longer bound to our physical body, and our spirit takes over. Becoming untethered from the body and led by the soul is an amazing experience. At our very core, the soul drives us to grow, achieve, search, and learn—all in a singular quest to become more. At some point, whether it's a business or a human, if the life force is squelched, the process of dying ensues.

We don't need to be in perfect health to grow. We don't need to have things work out the way we planned to learn from the experience.

We don't need to be successful to learn from failure any more than we need to fail to learn from success. But we do need to remain committed to growth. To do so means to always seek the lesson, focus on what we can learn, and look for the insight in the mundane facets of life as well as the transformational periods we experience. We are either growing or dying—the choice is ours, moment by moment.

To reap huge changes, personal growth must be more than a few minutes a day. It needs to be an active and intentional part of your day. Personal growth—not some master strategy—is the key to success. Why? Because when we're growing, we're expanding what's possible. We are more effective, persuasive, visionary, congruent, alive, joyful, and attractive. When we stay the same version of ourselves, doing the same thing over and over, life will 100 percent stay the same. People are *learning*, but unless they actively apply what they learn, they're not growing.

So, how do you know you're growing and not just learning? You make more money, have more freedom, hit your goals, and have more success. You take bigger risks and frequently find yourself outside of your comfort zone. It takes less time to do things than it used to—like handling conflict, deciding faster, and acting immediately. Your relationships in business and your personal life are way better, and you easily find people who are part of your tribe. You feel more whole, fulfilled, present, relaxed, and confident about your life as it is right now. The real you shows up more and more, unfiltered, congruent, authentic, humble, and vulnerable.

Making external changes will not change your internal being. You need greater self-awareness, self-compassion, a life audit of your goals, needs, presence, personality traits, values, and permanent behavioral change.

You don't get to stay the same—because everything changes. Businesses, relationships, and the human soul all change. They're either moving forward—growing—or dying. Consider a business that tries to stay the same in a changing world. No doubt it will have to shut its doors if it doesn't have an online presence or at least an email account. Relationships cannot stay the same. Either the individuals constantly and steadfastly work to make it better, or it fades and maybe even ends.

The human soul is no different. No one can stay the same. If you try to stay the same, if you refuse to develop yourself, if you don't practice being an ever-better human being, you're starving your soul, and it will die. Your body may not die. But your soul will wither, shriveling in on itself. Growth is as necessary for the human soul as it is for businesses and relationships.

> *"The real secret to a life of abundance is to stop spending your days searching for security and to start spending your time pursuing opportunity."*
>
> — Robin Sharma

EXERCISE

1. What will you do to expand yourself?

_____
_____
_____
_____
_____

2. How will you respond to growth opportunities?

_____
_____
_____
_____

3. Who are you going to follow to learn from?

_____
_____

4. Why do you want to grow?

_____
_____
_____

5. Write your personal growth plan for the next two years.

_____
_____
_____
_____
_____
_____
_____
_____

FIVE TIPS FOR GROWING

1. Start loving your growth journey; it will last a lifetime.
2. Know perfect doesn't exist; just be better today than yesterday.
3. Understand growth means patience and being kind to yourself.
4. Elevate your mindset and believe you deserve to be the best version of yourself.
5. Know when you grow, everything and everyone around you will grow too.

SUMMARY

Growth is not about being perfect. It's about ensuring it remains a work in progress. "I'm a mess, but I'm working on it!" Learning happens formally in school and workshops, but your best lessons come from the school of life. You can learn and grow from, and be inspired by, everyone you meet. And usually the most annoying coworker, the snail-slow customer service representative, the world's worst driver, the toughest student, or the most difficult child will help you grow the most. Each situation can bring out the best in you. But it's not a big deal if you're patient and forgiving, loving and caring within the situations in your life you enjoy the most.

Growth comes when you are patient and forgiving, loving and caring in the most challenging situations, with the most difficult people. All of life's moments hold lessons. Approach each situation with an open heart to have a growth mindset. The moment you feel your heart close to a situation, it's your cue: Time to grow!

Growing looks like choosing to be a better version of you. It is about acceptance, forgiveness, and compassion. It's about being courageous. It's about being strong but flexible. It's about listening, speaking from the heart and your truth, caring, and helping. It's about love. When you choose love, you grow.

> *"When you're not growing, you're dying."*
>
> — Tony Robbins

Growth can come from anything like feeding your mind with books, classes, or lectures. Or perhaps even just listening to others and the world around you. Growth can be taking a chance, a risk, or putting yourself in a situation beyond your comfort zone. It also may be pushing yourself and trying to find new ways to be a better version of yourself every single day. If you're a business owner, maybe it's finding new strategies or tactics to grow your business or investments. Or maybe it's learning a new language or skill. It could also be something simple like trying a new kind of food, seeing a different movie than you usually do, or pushing yourself not to settle for the known but to reach, instead, for the unknown. Life is growth. From the acorn to the oak, the puppy to the dog, the baby to the adult, all life starts small and grows into its full potential. Part of this growth is the growth of knowledge, skills, and an ability to handle and tackle the challenges of life.

> *"If you as a human being transform yourself,*
> *you affect the consciousness of the rest of the world."*
>
> — Krishnamurti

Ken Blanchard said:

> There's a difference between interest and commitment. When you're interested in doing something, you do it only when circumstances permit. Commitment is what keeps you going in the face of adversity and challenges. When you're committed to something, you accept no excuses, only results.

Commitment ignites action. Commitment is persistence with purpose. Commitment is respect.

> *"The need for security calls for a protector; achievement calls for a motivator; cooperation calls for a team builder; understanding calls for a nurturer; creativity calls for an innovator; moral values call for a transformer; spiritual fulfillment calls for a sage, or seer."*
>
> — Deepak Chopra

In eight areas of life, you have the power to let your soul guide you: thoughts, emotions, perception, personal relationships, social role, environment, speech, and your body. In all these areas, your behavior affects the people you lead. If you evolve, so will they. Leading from the soul means evolution is your top priority. You never act in a way that may lower the self-esteem of others. You examine your underlying beliefs and modify them as new opportunities for growth reveal themselves. Because evolution is an unstoppable force in the universe, you draw upon invisible powers. Therefore, being responsible is no longer a burden. It rests lightly on you if you continue to grow.

CALL TO ACTION

Look at your strengths and weaknesses. I challenge you to learn new skills and techniques to grow. Find a new perspective when you're challenged. Do not get attached to other people's growth path. See failing as the steppingstone for growth.

Chapter 16

Circle of Influence

"A mentor is someone who sees more talent and ability within you, than you see in yourself, and helps bring it out of you."

— Bob Proctor

What really matters to you? What does success look like to you? Where do you want your career or business to be in a year and five years? What will it take to get there? And critically, who do you need in your corner? Who will keep you accountable? Who is your example? Let me share with you some of the people who have inspired me to grow.

MY STORY

Finding the right mentors, coaches, and leaders is a lifelong journey. They will change when you change. I have had many mentors so far, and I'm committed to having many more. I truly believe the right mentor will show up when the time is right.

Many stories inspired me over my lifetime. Every virtual mentor, real life mentor, coach, author, and speaker who inspired me has added to my success and personal growth. Sometimes I learn from just one sentence, or their personal story, or the content they create. And they've all impressed me with their selfless, committed, giving, and motivating character that created a legacy for themselves, their generation, and many generations to come.

> *"It's time you realized that you have something in you more powerful and miraculous than the things that affect you and make you dance like a puppet."*
>
> — Marcus Aurelius

The first coach I personally hired was Nicole van Leeuwen, a life coach. Realizing I was pretty messed up, I knew I needed a coach. Now knowing you need a coach and taking action to find a good one are two different stories. I wasn't happy with myself nor my life, so I had two options, being a victim and staying miserable or putting on my big girl pants and facing my demons and past trauma to become happy, confident, and excited about life again. I wanted a different outcome in my life, my relationships, and my career. I only wanted to hire the best, and although I knew I had to go through some real mirrors and tough sessions, that's what I was committed to. It took me a long time to find a coach who totally understood me but also was strong enough to let me get away with my smarty pants and hiding moves, if you know what I mean. Many tears and sessions later, I started to feel more confident, my self-esteem started to blossom, and I gained a lot of clarity on who I am and who I was destined to be. Nicole was not just a coach; she did many regression sessions of reincarnation experiences, inner child embracings, and systemic work with me. We did many family constellations and breathwork, and she professionally guided me in every area of my life from spiritual to emotional and from mental to physical to heal the past, shine today, and love the future. Now this was not an overnight program. I spent several years going to her sessions, driving ninety minutes one way to be coached by the best I could find. She absolutely put a footprint on who I am today. As I always like to say, "Don't forget where you come from and who helped you to get where you are now." Nicole is one of my heroes in my book.

> *"We must find the time to stop and thank those people who make a difference in our lives."*
>
> — John F. Kennedy

Tony Robbins has been my mentor and virtual coach since 1998. Although back in the day, he only coached me via watching his DVDs, that helped me tremendously to get out of my shell and make it through tough times. Later, I went to his in-person events in London, and when I moved to the USA and my wife shared the stage with him, I repeatedly watched him speak in person. I always was front row taking notes, participating, and manifesting my desire to meet him in person one day. In 2018, Cheri and I were invited to take a picture with Tony, and they were magical seconds. We were not allowed to talk to him, but I knew in my gut that we would meet one day and have a conversation, and I would be able to tell my personal story. I've read all of Tony's books as hardcovers, and via Audible, I listened to his wisdom and inspiration over and over. Since 2020, I have been following him via YouTube and his Virtual Summits. When I have a tough day, a setback or I don't feel motivated, I always find a way to connect with Tony. He has helped me so much, even though we never sat once in a room together.

In 2024, I had the honor of being on an hour Zoom call with him and my wife Cheri Tree. We're still in conversation about some future possibilities. I'm manifesting to meet with him in person and even speak at one of his events. Everything is possible! And as of today, I'm still listening weekly to Tony for my dose of inspiration and tapping into my highest self to keep getting better every day. Tony Robbins is a number-one *New York Times* bestselling author and the nation's number-one life and business strategist. He has impacted millions with his life-changing events. He's been named in the top fifty of *Worth Magazine's* 100 most powerful people in global finance for three consecutive years, been honored by Harvard Business Press as one of the Top 200 Business Gurus, and by American Express as one of the Top Six Business Leaders in the World to coach its entrepreneurial clients. *Fortune's* cover article named him the "CEO Whisperer." That's why leaders call upon him to help them lead.

> *"I believe life is constantly testing us for our level of commitment, and life's greatest rewards are reserved for those who demonstrate a never-ending commitment to act until they achieve. This level of resolve can move mountains, but it must be constant and consistent."*
>
> — Tony Robbins

In 2005, I met my first business coach, Vera Renema. She was the Founder and CEO of Finace BV in Amstelveen, the Netherlands. I remember the day I met her like yesterday. She invited me for an interview after I was recommended by a recruiting agency. After Vera said, "Welcome," she immediately let me know my resume didn't make any sense, and she was curious to find out who was behind it. We had a great conversation, and she hired me as a business unit director for Finace BV. She gave me an opportunity to resurrect this unit from death and make it profitable again. I guess she had nothing to lose! Little did she know about my commitment, determination, resilience, and winning mentality. My first day was a shocker. Nobody to guide me, help me, or answer any questions. I was off on my own after I received my car keys, my laptop, and my phone and was guided to my office where I literally only found a desk and a chair. No clue what to do, I decided to walk into other offices to introduce myself and ask for guidance and collaboration. No luck because I had entered a very competitive environment with 95 percent men. After my first week, I decided to ask Vera for a meeting. That was the moment I asked if she was willing to mentor me and meet with me weekly. Once she committed to meeting with me, I started to get traction in my unit. I worked with my colleagues, and I picked up the phone and made endless cold calls to hopefully get an appointment. Suddenly, success kicked in. Several projects got assigned to my unit, and off we went. Vera started to invite me to business lunches. I listened and took notes. She asked me questions like, "What would you do in this situation?" I learned most by listening to her conversations with CEOs and Executives of Fortune 500 companies. I became an incredible listener, and she taught me to ask great questions and then be quiet. I became very successful, and my business unit started to thrive. She mentored me to become a great businesswoman who was able to sit at any table and be invited into any room. Eighteen months later, she sold the company, and I followed her to her new venture. Soon, I realized I wanted to be my own boss, build my own business, and enjoy the freedom of being an entrepreneur. She supported me. She always believed in my talents, gifts, and ability to succeed against all odds. Her mentorship set me up for the success I have now.

> *"True mentors have this unique ability to pick up vibes that everyone else misses from within you."*
>
> — Ahmad R Kazi

When you're ready, the opportunity and mentor show up. That's how I met my mentor, Cheri Tree, who later became my wife in 2013. When I met Cheri, I bought her BANK training for my consulting business to help me understand my personal relationships better. Soon, I understood the power of this methodology and I became a certified trainer and reseller. Cheri was looking for someone to open the European market, and I said, "I'm the one." After my first Codebreaker Summit in the Netherlands, I asked her if she wanted to mentor me. I started to listen to all USA calls, mostly in the middle of the night my time. I flew from Amsterdam to Palm Springs, San Diego, and Las Vegas to see her speak in person. The first five years, I never missed a live speaking gig or training by Cheri. She's one the best female speakers and trainers in the world. When I was still living in the Netherlands, I showed up as much as I could virtually. As soon as I moved to the USA, I joined her in every meeting, at every event, and at every dinner we had with clients, relationships, and partners. Cheri taught me so much on Why They Buy, about the sales process, converting from stage, personal branding, and having a millionaire mindset. Along the way, she started to put me on stage with her, either for a testimonial or a story. Later, I became one of her main trainers to teach the BANK system and provide trainer certification at Codebreaker Technologies' hosted events. Cheri taught me how to engage the room and run the sales table or showcase booth at an event. Besides her mentorship in becoming a great trainer and speaker, she also taught me to have resilience, faith, and patience. Faith and patience were two areas I especially had to improve, and still today, patience is my big growth area. Cheri taught me through the lens of BANK to be less judgmental, have more understanding of people, and to meet them at their level of understanding themselves and others. Cheri is an incredible mentor and business coach for business owners, entrepreneurs, salespeople, and speakers. She has mastered how to influence people and move them to take action in every area of life and business. She mentored me to become a great speaker and trainer. Cheri Tree is a best-selling author, professional keynote speaker, and world-renowned entrepreneur and innovator. She is the Founder and CEO of Codebreaker Technologies, with Codebreakers in more than one-hundred countries worldwide. She is the creator of the revolutionary BANK methodology and Codebreakers' patented Personality Coding Technology and Artificial Intelligence.

"Why your prospects buy is exponentially more important than how you sell. That's why sales is not a numbers game, but a people game."

— Cheri Tree

Robin Sharma became my mentor during my corporate career starting in 2006 when I began to read his books. I have read all of his incredible books. His book *The 5 AM Club* changed my life and my daily routines. Two of his latest books, *The Everyday Hero Manifesto* and *The Wealth Money Can't Buy* are incredible for helping every busy entrepreneur and business owner to really dial into what's most important and learn how to balance life, health, business, and relationships.

In 2022, I signed up for his virtual training platform with hundreds of hours of incredible content on leadership, daily routines, and creating a life you desire. I watched every video and started to implement a lot of his wisdom and teachings in my life and business. In 2023, I joined his private Mastermind Group with thirty high-level, very successful business owners from around the world. Being in a room with incredible human beings and Robin's presence changed my direction and my priorities for the remaining half of my life. I built friendships and power partnerships for life, which is an experience nobody can ever take away. When my mastermind ended, I asked Robin to speak at our annual ICONIC conference for Codebreaker Technologies and he said, "Yes."

In January 2024, Robin delivered a very powerful keynote about world-class leadership to our Codebreaker Community. When you suddenly share the stage with your own mentor, things shift to another level. My energy shifted as did my focus, intention, presence, and commitment to my personal life goals and life purpose. Every week, I listen to a chapter of one of his books and watch some of his great videos with powerful content.

Robin Sharma is considered to be one of the top five leadership experts in the world as well as an internationally acclaimed bestselling author.

His work is embraced by rock stars, royalty, billionaires, and celebrity CEOs.

"The smallest of actions is always better than the noblest of intentions. Change is hardest at the beginning, messiest in the middle, and best at the end. Dreamers are mocked as impractical. The truth is they are the most practical, as their innovations lead to progress and a better way of life for all of us."

— Robin Sharma

LESSONS LEARNED

Inspiration comes from the outside. Connect with people who inspire you. Read biographies, and listen to podcasts or audiobooks to connect with your heroes. They can be authors, speakers, athletes, activists, coaches, company owners, consultants, world leaders, or even your friends.

When someone inspires you, it will fuel your motivation. Inspiration will ignite your fire, and you will be able to motivate yourself to follow your dreams and desires. Motivation comes from the inside, but we all need that outside inspiration to become better and keep showing up in the world.

Selecting an in-person mentor should be a thoughtful, reflective, and intentional process. A mentor is not just an advisor and coach, but also an ally, a raving fan, and even a friend. Know what you want out of the relationship. What is the desired outcome of this investment in yourself? If you aren't honest with yourself about what you want to achieve with a mentor, you will waste time and energy and may even find yourself on a path that doesn't serve you. It's perfectly normal to be uncertain about what you want to accomplish. And it's okay, good even, to adjust your goals as you and they evolve. But if you don't have a vision for your future, the advice you get will be empty and unhelpful. You don't need a finished painting to begin seeking a mentor, but you do need a first draft. Meaning, be clear on your why, mission, vision, values, and the results you're looking for.

I think a mentor must, above all else, believe in you and your goals. Having a mentor who has been where you are, understands the challenges ahead, and has already navigated over, around, and under them will make a world of difference. Your mentor should share your values and be just as fiercely committed to them. If you aren't aligned when it comes to your aspirations and the steps you intend to take along the way, you risk getting the wrong advice. The same is true for you as well, by the way; you need a mentor you believe in! As I often say, "Stop taking advice from people more messed up than you." Your mentor can save you thirty years of failure and mistakes. When you hire a mentor, their hourly rate is not based on the hour itself; it's based on their twenty-plus years of experience and expertise that will save you time, energy, and money now and long term.

Emotional intelligence (EQ) is probably the most important quality for both leaders and mentors. A mentor with high EQ can effectively navigate your emotions, uncover your blind spots, and provide insightful feedback that fosters self-awareness and growth. You want a mentor with empathy who can guide you through it, whatever "it" is.

I also look for spiritual intelligence (SQ). Do they have a strong connection to the Divine Source and their own soul desire? Align with someone who lives the life, has obtained the business results, and has the personal relationships you're looking for. Find a mentor with a collaborative mindset who wants you to win big and will help you to get there.

"Most people don't have an intention issue, but they lack strategy and execution on their dreams and goals. That is why they get distracted easily and live the same life for seventy-five years."

— Esther Wildenberg

EXERCISE

1. What life do you want?

_____
_____
_____
_____
_____

2. What do you want to get out of mentorship?

_____
_____
_____

3. What obstacles are you trying to overcome?

_____
_____
_____

4. What are you excited about right now?

_____
_____
_____

5. What did/didn't you like about a previous mentor?

_____
_____
_____
_____

FIVE TIPS FOR FINDING YOUR MENTOR

1. Define the goals you want a mentor to help you with. Write them in your journal.
2. Determine whether your prospective mentor has chemistry with you.
3. Find common ground, values, presence, personality, and alignment with your potential mentor.
4. Check out their record of success. Experience and expertise are key.
5. Ask someone you know and trust—someone who has been mentored, is growing, and whose business is growing too—for a referral.

SUMMARY

I have been inspired by many great legends. The stories above are just a few. What they all have in common is they refused to give up on their dreams and soul desire of making a difference in the world and/or being the first to do something the world ridiculed them for. Many of these legends changed sports, music, politics, business, and life. They paved the path for our generation, showing us what's possible when you don't let anyone stop you. One person can change humanity.

Mentors can make a huge difference. I have hired mentors and coaches since I was twenty-four in my personal life and career. It was the best money I ever spent.

In 1998, I started watching and listening to Tony Robbins. He has truly been my number-one virtual mentor for twenty-six years. Over the past two decades, I have seen him at his events and on many stages we shared over the years. I always stay to hear Robbins. In 2024, I had the blessing and honor to having an hour-long, in-person Zoom call with him. I already loved him, and he helped me tremendously.

After the call, all I can say is he's one of the most humble, positive, kind, complimentary, and loving men I have ever met. I use a lot of his lessons, and he's one of the keystones of my personal growth. As of today, I still listen to his audiobooks and follow his virtual events. I'm manifesting an in-person meeting with him one day.

In 2022, I joined Robin Sharma's personal mastermind with twenty-nine other successful business owners from around the world. It was an incredible experience to be in a room with him and so many wonderful people, all with one goal—to become better and better by giving back, growing, and balancing our lives. This was a yearlong mastermind program starting in 2023, and it was the best investment in myself and exactly what I needed. When Sharma spoke at our company conference in 2024, he inspired our community to start living the life they desire and balance all forms of wealth. He is an introvert and a little shy, but he has incredible wisdom and a unique gift for deconstructing complex theories into simple methods and systems. I have read all his books more than once, and he will continue to be an inspiration and source via his virtual learning platform.

Besides these well-known mentors, I have hired many coaches and mentors, and they have all contributed to my growth. At the time, they were each perfect for me. I believe we all need coaches and mentors in our personal lives and careers to get the results we want and live our best life. The best investment is the one in yourself.

The best part of being connected to great mentors is their circle of influence, their community, and opportunities to collaborate. When you have the right mentor, many doors will open for you. It's an investment that will give you an ROI (return-on-investment) and ROT (return-on-time).

"In the infinity of life where I am, all is perfect, whole, and complete, I no longer choose to believe in old limitations and lack. I now choose to begin to see myself as the Universe sees me—perfect, whole, and complete."

— Louise Hay

CALL TO ACTION

I challenge you to clarify your life and business goals. Hire a mentor to help you reach the growth you desire. Make a list of people who inspire you. Live your dreams and become the next legend, even if it's just in your own family. I encourage you to become a mentor for others.

Chapter 17

Your Identity

"Motherhood brings as much joy as ever, but it still brings boredom, exhaustion, and sorrow too. Nothing else will ever make you as happy or as sad, as proud or as tired, for nothing is quite as hard as helping a person develop his own individuality especially while you struggle to keep your own."

— Marguerite Kelly

"If you're a twin, you know your sibling is the best thing and the worst thing to ever happen to you. Being a twin means spending your life arguing about who is the original and who is the remix."

— Esther Wildenberg

Have you ever felt lost? Have ever questioned who you are?" Have you ever lost your identity? Did someone ever try to change you? Have you ever wondered why you're here right now? Do you know who you truly are? Determining my own special identity was not easy. It isn't for most people. But when you're a twin, there's a whole added level of difficulty. Let me share with you two of my biggest struggles with finding and retaining my identity.

MY STORY

Being an identical twin and becoming a mom at forty-six made me struggle with my identity....

Losing Your Identity as an Identical Twin

Starting life together is an exceptional experience most don't get to feel. My sister Nicole was always there with me, right from the first cells to being born. She was always a playmate, and we experienced the same nerves on our first day of school. I always had someone to play with when my friends weren't home or on a rainy Sunday afternoon. Even on days when I should have been the center of attention, like my birthday, there was always another person to think about. So, it was never "my" birthday; it was always "our" birthday. It was never "my" gift; it was always "our" gift to share. Even when we turned eighteen, people gave us a gift to share.

Nicole is six minutes older than me. She had a six-minute head start in the world. We are genetically identical—as we formed from the same egg, which then split in the womb—however, at seventeen, we went on our own journeys and found our own identities, our own friends, career, and partners. And we have totally different personalities.

People still get us mixed up. I got called Nicole daily. There are just as many differences between us as there are similarities. While we have very similar faces, I was always slightly taller than Nicole growing up, although she always mentioned right away that she was the oldest. The six minutes were a big deal, at least when we were young. Of course, the more time you spend with us, the easier it is to tell us apart. But being told apart was also a choice. We tried to look different. We believed we looked different, until we heard again: Who's Esther? Who's Nicole? Who's the oldest? Who's the smartest? Who is the kindest? Who is better at (fill in the blank)? This could go on and on.

When I came downstairs in the morning and saw Nicole in a similar outfit to mine, I would rush back to my room to change. The funny thing is, when we went shopping as teenagers, each with our own friends, we mostly came home with the same clothes, except I always bought less but paid more.

I've spent a lot of my life being treated like a dress-up doll. Birthday presents would come in the form of matching outfits, which we were then expected to wear at the same time, as if we were an art exhibit for people to point at and take photos of. "Aww, don't twins look cute when they're dressed the same?" It's not cute. It's annoying. Even today I don't like to wear the same clothes as Nicole or my partner. Nicole lives in the Netherlands, so the chance is less than 1 percent I'll wear the same clothes. But my partner Cheri likes to match clothes—you can guess how that goes.

As kids, Nicole was considered more of a tomboy than I was. We are both lesbian, and we still have a lot of similarities, still look the same, only we live completely different lives. Not better or worse, just different. Of course, we are very similar—I can't argue with that. When you spend half your life with someone, you're probably going to have a lot in common. We understand each other and have the same sense of humor. I can normally tell if something's bothering her, or when she's lying, even now, when I live in the United States and Nicole lives in the Netherlands. We often talk in disjointed sentences—we know what the other is going to say. But I am still my own person. Just like other siblings may be similar, or two close-knit people in a relationship, you still recognize the people involved as their own entities.

As a twin, you must accept that, conjoined or not, you will always be joined at the hip. You must accept that you come as a package—unknown at school, getting praised for things your twin did, and getting in trouble for things you had not done. Teachers were often confused and sometimes we took advantage of it. It was easy to outsmart the education system. I was never referred to as just myself—it was always plural—the twins. And when someone does attempt to stamp a name on me, it's a fifty-fifty chance they'll get it right. But that doesn't really bother me. If someone simply slips up and calls me Nicole, I understand; it's easy to do. By calling me "one of the twins," you're dismissing me as an individual. You're shrugging off my entire identity as if it's no big deal.

I also have a younger sister, Claire, who had to deal with her two older twin sisters. We didn't make her childhood easy, and I have a lot of compassion for her. We got a lot of attention and the four-year-age difference was hard on her. She literally was the third wheel on the wagon. I know now we hurt her a lot back in the day when we were just children and annoying teenagers. I have a good relationship with Claire now, and the older we get, the more we understand ourselves, our journey, and the things we did, not to harm but just to figure out who we were.

Growing up is hard. Struggling through your teens when you're supposed to be "finding yourself" comes with more pressure when you're constantly compared to someone else. You're trying to work out who you are, when your every action is cross-referenced with someone else who is stumbling through their own problems. Being a twin is odd because you have to take responsibility for someone else's actions as well as your own. A group of people disliked me at college after my sister got in a fight. They knew it wasn't me, but they admitted they just couldn't trust me either.

Comparison is so counterintuitive—when all you really want to do is make yourself the person you want to be. I just want to be me. Sharing takes on a whole new meaning when you're a twin. Who needs the chicken and the egg when you've got the age-old question—who was born first?

And I believe the Universe knew Nicole wouldn't know what to do without me, so it made sure we entered the world together. It's an agreement we signed up for before coming to Earth. It's part of the journey and lessons we chose. When you have identical twins in your life, just know the identical twin struggle is real—and so is their unconditional lifelong bond!

Losing Your Identity by Becoming a Mom

> *"Motherhood is a choice you make every day, to put someone else's happiness and well-being ahead of your own, to teach the hard lessons, to do the right thing even when you're not sure what the right thing is…and to forgive yourself, over and over again, for doing everything wrong."*
>
> — Donna Ball

So much joy surrounds the birth of a new baby. You're pregnant as a couple (or single), you make the announcement, and anticipation builds. The new life grows inside your swollen belly. Preparations are made. Rooms are decorated. Friends and family gather to celebrate at baby showers. Then, the day arrives. Your new baby enters the world. Absolute delight surrounds birth. Experiencing the first moments of the miracle of life is unforgettable. Life changes in the blink of an eye. With that one final push, you are a mom.

Your story may look different. Your life might have changed as you gathered the new member of your family from the arms of a brave woman who knew she couldn't care for the child the way you would be able to. Maybe your life was transformed as your feet crossed the threshold of an orphanage on the other side of the world. Whatever your journey, life changed when you became a mom.

For some, it was a seamless transition. You always knew you wanted to be a mom. The new life completed a puzzle, although the journey was tough at times. For me it was a rebirth, and for Cheri a completion. It changed me, though, and I wasn't sure I liked the change. Don't get me wrong. I loved Kai from the first moment, even way before. I delighted in him. Staring at him was my favorite pastime. Cheri and I watched each other change and celebrated each milestone. We took four- or five-hour shifts driving to the NICU (neonatal intensive care unit) to have skin-to-skin time with him. When Kai came home, we both shifted into our new reality. I wanted the best for him. But in this new life, I also wanted me.

I was independent, adventurous, and fun. I used to be the one jumping off cliffs, going on spontaneous trips, doing things in my own time on my terms. But now I was grounded. I felt stuck. Everyone was in lockdown during COVID. We were not allowed to be together with Kai at the NICU. The first six weeks of his life were spent in an incubator and just having one-on-one time with each mommy. He was surrounded by angels and amazing nurses. They all deserve an award for "love." When they take away your freedom, your ability to see people, it's like putting you in prison. Kai was born in an energetic time of fear and mass manipulation. We had no help from family, nannies, or any other help the first six months Kai was home. And I felt lonely every day.

At the same time, we had to pivot our company when a whole community was relying on us to keep the company growing and thriving. We did pivot in a beautiful way, but it took a lot of our time and energy that we couldn't put into our relationship. Our relationship started to have some cracks. I believe we're still together because of our strong five-year foundation before we got pregnant and had Kai. The past few years were hard, lonely, and challenging in many ways. We're both wired very positively so we kept working on finding our new "relationship." I had to let go of what was and replace it with something new.

Life would never be the same, and so it changed me, our relationship, our business, and our life. Kai's godmother has been our angel and best friend the past seven years. She was the glue between all of us, reminding us about our individuality, our love, our mission, the gift of Kai, the beauty of growing and learning with him, and the opportunity to share an amazing story with the world. We renewed our vows in the spring of 2024, and we're creating a new love story, a new relationship, and a deeper connection.

As a new mom, I felt my wings had been clipped. No longer did I feel like my carefree self. I had responsibilities. A little human being was depending on me for survival. Eventually, he would depend on me for teaching, security, and discipline, too. My story is not finished. I am not finished. I'm a work in progress. I'm not the me I was five years ago before I had Kai, but I am not lost. I'm still here being refined and reworked. Life has a whole new meaning and purpose. Something beautiful is happening. I have the opportunity to teach Kai the life lessons I learned. I can show him the world and introduce him to people, cultures, and languages. I can show him we're all one. We're all love. We're all here to make the world a better place. We all have a purpose. We all have something special and unique to give that no one else has, not even my twin sister Nicole!

"Motherhood is about raising and celebrating the child you have, not the child you wish you had. And celebrating the mom you are, not the mom you thought you had to be."

— Esther Wildenberg

LESSONS LEARNED

Identity is not something we find; it is something we create. Sometimes, the only way to find yourself is to get lost. We are not defined by our past or our future, but by the choices we make in the present. To be lost is not a sign of weakness, but a sign of courage to explore the unknown. Sometimes, the greatest adventure is the one that takes place within yourself. Your identity is not limited by society's expectations, but by your own imagination. It's having the courage to let go of "what was" and discover a "new version" of you.

Identity includes the many relationships people cultivate, such as their identity as a child, friend, partner, and parent. It involves external characteristics over which a person has little or no control, such as height, race, or socioeconomic class. Identity also encompasses political opinions, moral attitudes, and religious beliefs, all of which guide the choices one makes daily. People who are overly concerned with the impression they make, or who feel a core aspect of themselves, such as gender or sexuality, is not being expressed, can struggle acutely with their identity. Reflecting on the discrepancy between who one is and who one wants to be can be a powerful catalyst for change.

"Having a well-developed sense of self is hugely beneficial in helping us make choices in life. From something as small as favorite foods to larger concerns like personal values, knowing what comes from our own self versus what comes from others allows us to live authentically."

— Erika Myers

I found myself when I realized it is okay to do things for me. I was under the false impression that becoming a mom meant life had to be all about my son. Yes, we do become more selfless—a good thing—when we become parents. However, it is important and healthy to remember what makes you tick and allow yourself the freedom to pursue those things. I found myself when I fought to find myself. I didn't want to be the person I had become. I didn't want to feel sad, always searching for joy. This captivity was unacceptable. One of the big phrases in our family is "Be happy and be kind." I chose it as a family motto because I needed the reminder. I didn't want to lie down and wallow in self-pity. Acknowledging I was unhappy and could change my attitude was key to my rebirth.

I can't say I've arrived. I have a feeling it will be a lifelong process, but I can feel the phoenix beginning to rise. I needed to change. Impatience and pride were all key things I needed to work on. And I still struggle to be patient. Parenting humbled me. It became a mirror, showing me the sins that needed to be exposed and behaviors that needed to be modified. Parenting is teaching me to live more in wonder. It's testing my patience. I was a fabulous partner, friend, and leader, so my pride has been addressed at every turn. I lost myself when I became a mom, but I'm finding a new me—a better me—as I rise from the dark back into the light.

> *"Motherhood is the greatest thing and the hardest thing."*
> — Ricki Lake

EXERCISE

1. Have you ever felt like you lost your identity?
_____
_____
_____

2. When you let go of the past, what will your new story be?
_____
_____
_____
_____
_____

3. What dreams do you have?

_____
_____
_____
_____
_____
_____
_____
_____

4. What expectations do you have?

_____
_____
_____
_____

5. Are you ready to put yourself first so you can be a more optimized you? What are your action steps?

_____
_____
_____

FIVE TIPS FOR FINDING YOUR (NEW) IDENTITY

1. Focus on your strengths.
2. Do things that make you happy.
3. Make your own choices.
4. Go on a retreat with like-minded people.
5. Accept labels like mom, sister, daughter, etc.

SUMMARY

We all face moments when we feel we have lost our identity—such as when we break up with a partner, go through a divorce, lose our only child, go through bankruptcy, or lose a job. When a big event happens in your life, you can feel like you're losing your identity. I did. And I learned to love myself in the process and realized I didn't lose my identity—I gained a new one. You can have it all and be all as long as you identify with what feels best for you.

> *"In the egoic state, your sense of self, your identity, is derived from your thinking mind—in other words, what your mind tells you about yourself: the storyline of you, the memories, the expectations, all the thoughts that go through your head continuously and the emotions that reflect those thoughts. All those things make up your sense of self."*
>
> — Eckhart Tolle

When Kai was born, I wrote vows for Kai. I share them with you because I believe our role as parents is to guide our child the best we can to prepare them to become incredible, loving, kind, successful, happy, and open-minded grownups who will change the world for the better in a positive, high vibration way.

Kai—

I love you with all I am.

I promise,

I will always take care of you, support you, protect you, and mentor you through life the best I can.

I will learn from you every day from the day you were born. You gave my life a new perspective. Looking through your eyes and how you explore the world makes me feel happy and curious again.

Your beautiful soul and how your smile touches every heart is breathtaking and special.

You're my biggest challenge and lesson in this lifetime. You came into our family for a reason. You chose us.

You're my biggest love, and I'm proud of you every day. I will cheer for you to become the best version of you every day.

You will change many lives as you already do today with your deep blue eyes and gorgeous smile. You shine light and love into this world.

You can become anyone and anything you want. You can achieve any dream or goal you set. I promise I will always be your biggest fan.

You're sweet, kind, smart, handsome, funny, and curious. Life is a journey, and we will walk it together until you're ready to fly out of our nest. And even then, I'll always be your safe place, your Mimi.

And when I'm a shining Star in the sky or an Angel, I'll guide you and protect you from the other side.

I love you unconditionally,

Mimi Esther

You can have it all; you can do it all. You can be a present, loving partner. You can be a great, unconditional mom. You can be a business owner and entrepreneur. You can be a good employee. You can be an amazing friend. You can be a humanitarian. You can travel the world. You can go to parties and seminars. You can go for beach walks by yourself. You can take care of yourself. You can join a sports club or a team. You can go on a silent retreat or business mastermind. You can have it all. You can do it all.

When you practice, "after me, you come first," and plan your day, week, month, and year according to your dreams and expectations, you can live your best life!

> *"I can imagine no heroism greater than motherhood."*
>
> — Lance Conrad

CALL TO ACTION

Define your values and live by them. I encourage you to spend time alone. Smile a lot and shine your light. Love who you are—you're perfect the way you are. Believe you're the best version of you. Don't be attached to what others think of you. That's their journey.

Chapter 18

Create a Legacy

"Be the change you wish to see in the world."

— Mahatma Gandhi

Do you ever think creatively about leaving a legacy? Did you know you can leave a unique legacy? Are you aware of the endless opportunities to leave a legacy? What if you could create a modern family with unconditional love outside your own home? Have you ever thought about the lives you can bless by being generous and creative? As we come to the end of this book, I want to share with you the legacy I hope to leave behind when I am gone from this world.

MY STORY

We're living in an interesting time. And there are several ways to look at the world and what is happening. I decided a few years ago not to engage in social media or post anything related to religion, politics, and mass media. Social media made me unhappy, and I realized I was part of the problem, creating separation and dividing people when I posted my opinion. We're all one, and I really don't care about who you vote for, your skin color, your sexual preferences, or what you're eating for breakfast.

I started to look into my own life more and the future I wanted for myself, our family, and Kai. My wife Cheri and I got pregnant via IVF. We spent three years looking for the right sperm donor. We were very picky because his DNA would affect Kai's future—not just his looks, but his genetics, athletic abilities, intelligence, health, eye color, hair color, etc. We also looked for a sperm donor with a personality that would fit our family dynamics and lifestyle.

And Cheri really wanted a chin dimple. When you can choose, why not create your perfect designer baby! We found him.

Another criterion was that by the time Kai turned eighteen, he would know the donor. Every child wants to know where they came from, how, and who gave them which traits.

Kai was our second pregnancy. He's our rainbow baby. During our first pregnancy, the fetus decided to clone himself by creating Baby B, his identical twin brother. We lost them at ten weeks, and we were devasted. When you hear and see their heartbeat, they take over your whole heart with a world of feelings and emotions.

After a nine-month break, we decided to go for round two, so we did on 11/11/2019 at 11:11 a.m. It was a very special moment full of hope, fear, excitement, and faith. We had to wait two weeks to know if we were pregnant. The day Cheri took the pregnancy test, I was flying to Spain to host a weeklong retreat with a group of women from the United States. I was in the air when Cheri got the results. The eleven-hour flight felt like weeks—time moves so slowly when you just want to know something. My patience was tested, but it was just one of many moments when I needed patience.

As soon as the plane landed, I turned on my phone to see Cheri's message.

Yes, we were pregnant!

I had to keep it a secret, because we decided not to tell anyone until we passed the one-hundred-day mark of the pregnancy. My mom was the only one we told right away. She was over the moon excited for us, and she was a great support during the pregnancy. Although she lives in the Netherlands, we were in touch daily and shared every doctor's appointment and update with her so she felt included even if we were in California.

On Valentine's Day 2020, we revealed the gender. We were pregnant with a boy, and we already loved him to the moon and back. We had the privilege of choosing the gender, and we both wanted a boy. He was growing strong and healthy with a nice, strong heartbeat.

At twenty-six weeks, Cheri had to go on bedrest, and my mommy journey started. It was right when COVID started, so we had no outside help at all. I was running the company and anticipating our new direction as we got ready for Kai's arrival.

We planned a virtual baby shower, and our dear friend, Kai's godmother, came to help with all the gifts. Our Amazon driver wondered what our *new* business was. I was overwhelmed by the 280-plus boxes of gifts for Kai. We felt so much support and love flowing through every gift and message. It truly was a day we will never forget. For days, we worked on unwrapping the gifts and organizing Kai's room.

And then the surprise—at twenty-nine-and-a half weeks, Cheri's water broke. That was very early. We got to the hospital around 5 p.m. on May 23. That's when the journey of contractions and pain began.

Cheri had contractions every five minutes. The doctors gave her medicine to slow the contractions, and by 11 p.m., they had slowed to every forty-five minutes. The doctors told me it was okay to go home to Polo, our dog, and our friend Angie, who magically arrived that afternoon at four. After triple-checking with Cheri, I went home for some food and to get fresh clothes and stuff for her.

Within an hour of getting home, Cheri called. All I heard was, "We're having a baby! Come!" Click. I rushed to my car and drove as fast as I safely could. I didn't even know what time it was. Then, I got a message from the Divine: Kai is born.

I knew it. I had missed his birth, his entrance into this world. I looked at the clock in my car. It was 1:05 a.m., May 24, 2020.

I parked in the first spot I saw and ran my legs from underneath my body to get in to Cheri and Kai as fast as I could. Once I entered the hospital, a security guard needed to test my temperature, ask all kinds of questions, print a name tag, and call to make sure my wife was having a baby. At this point my blood was boiling. As soon as the gate opened, I ran to the elevator. The security guard yelled that he had to walk me to the elevator. I yelled back, "Sorry. My wife is having a baby! I'm in a hurry."

What happened between when I left around eleven and getting back around 1:20 a.m. is Cheri went to sleep for a little bit. Then she woke up and felt an urgent need to pee. She called the nurse to assist with all the equipment attached to her and Kai. She sat down and nothing came out. The nurse suggested they check Cheri's bladder. The test showed Cheri's bladder was full. She tried to pee again, and a little bit came out. Shortly thereafter, Cheri had to go pee again and went to the bathroom. Nothing came out, but her body started to push and push. Cheri decided to do her own little research on what was happening with her body; she put her hand up in her vagina and held Kai's head in her hand. She called the nurse, who responded, "That's impossible."

What else could it be? A tennis ball, a peach? Cheri went to lay down and the nurse called the doctor. The OBGYN arrived in less than a minute, checked, and told Cheri, "You're going to have a baby."

In just a few minutes, the room was transformed into an operating room, with lights, trays, and monitors.

Cheri asked, "Shall I call my wife now?"

After calling me, Cheri asked for the epidural. The doctor said, "Uh-uh. Too late. Push."

Kai arrived in three pushes with his eyes wide open and letting everyone know his lungs were fine.

When I walked into the room, Kai was already in his incubator with his eyes wide open, tucked in, and not in need of an oxygen mask. Kai stared at me, saying with his eyes, "Mimi, I'm here; everything is okay." I took a lot of pictures quickly, then turned to Cheri to check if she was okay.

Cheri was bleeding like crazy—I mean like crazy. As the staff worked on her, I gave Cheri a kiss and went with the nurses to the NICU where they would do all the tests and get Kai settled in his incubator—his first experiences in this life.

After maybe thirty minutes, a nurse came running into Kai's room to rush me back to Cheri. When I walked into Cheri's delivery room, I saw the OBGYN's arm in her and pulling hard to get her placenta out. Blood was gushing out of Cheri, and she was a pale light gray. I saw light above her head as I took her hand, saying, "Come back. Stay here." Cheri came back slowly. She was white as the sheets. Taking the OBGYN's arm, I told him to keep Cheri alive. They moved Cheri to the operating room to do a D&C (dilation and curettage) to remove the placenta. I went back to the NICU to be with Kai, just staring at him for I don't know how long.

I called my mom in the Netherlands with the news that her grandson was born and doing great. I cried when I told Mom Cheri's situation. Mom was a great support, which was great because she was nine hours ahead in the Netherlands. For most of my friends, it was 2 a.m. so they were sleeping.

Finally, an hour later, Cheri was moved to the recovery room, where I got see her. It was an emotional moment; I had almost lost my wife. We celebrated Kai; I showed her the pictures.

> *"A grateful heart is a magnet for miracles."*
>
> — Jane Fuller

I'm deeply sad I missed Kai's birth and was not there for Cheri. I would only get this moment once. I had to work through my emotions. But all that really mattered was Kai and Cheri were both healthy and alive.

Kai was in the NICU for six weeks. The nurses were absolute angels. Having a baby during COVID was not fun for any of us. We were not allowed to be with Kai at the same time. For six weeks, I did the morning shift from 8 a.m. until 1 p.m. and Cheri from 1:30 p.m. until 6 p.m. Kai had an average of eight hours skin-to-skin time with us. He was thriving. Kai was a trooper, and he came home after six weeks, still four weeks before his due date. He was 3.11 pounds at birth, and 6.2 pounds when he came home. He was such a little nugget.

The journey of being a mom had begun. Dang, that's the hardest thing I have ever done. We missed all the becoming a parent courses because of COVID. We had one goal—keeping Kai alive. We had no help from family, friends, or neighbors. No nannies or cleaners available out of scarcity. Good luck, Mommies; here you go. Pivoting our company, no sleep, taking care of a baby, and keeping the home going. But life was still pure joy, full of unconditional love but freaking hard at times.

All moms know what I'm talking about. Polo was intrigued by Kai, not sure yet if she was happy about him. She adapted to the new situation fast, protecting and loving Kai. But she still did all she could to get my focused attention for just her. I'm not lying when I say that 2020, 2021, and 2022 were the hardest years of my life. Having Kai was wonderful, but not being able to travel, to see our family and friends, or get any help was devastating for us. We survived, and Kai is the most beautiful gift in our lives.

But we didn't want the journey to end with Kai. Cheri asked if I wanted another child. I was very clear about only wanting Kai. It had been a traumatic experience, and I didn't want to risk our family. Then the fertility clinic called and emailed to ask if we were willing to donate or sell back our twelve embryos. Cheri and I had several conversations about this emotional topic. Kai had twelve frozen brothers and sisters. We decided to create a legacy for Kai beyond his two mommies. We donated the embryos to the clinic under two conditions: 1. The families who got our embryos had to write us a letter and send us pictures. 2. The families had to agree to be in contact with us and let Kai build a relationship with his siblings living with these families.

We're very excited Kai has a pretty sister who just looks like him—yes, with a chin dimple and two brothers who are little Mini-Mes of Kai. When they're all together, it's fun to see the similarities and differences. The children each have a third of the egg, a third of the sperm, and a third of the mom who carried the baby. They all have different personality types. They are all very special and loved, and the families are beautiful people. We're excited and grateful we could create a new, modern family. It's the legacy that matters most. When we transition to the other side, Kai has a family he can count on. It's a legacy of unconditional love and family!

> "The greatest legacy you can leave to your kids are happy memories. Legacy is not leaving something for them; it's leaving something in them. Your story is the greatest legacy you will leave them. It's the longest-lasting legacy you will ever leave."
>
> — Esther Wildenberg

LESSONS LEARNED

Life always takes you where you're supposed to go. I often forget that. So, I remind myself. Often. Especially when it takes me into a challenge I sure as hell would rather not deal with or take responsibility for. So, I remind myself: If I'm facing a challenge, it means I'm ready for it. My whole life is made up of a string of broken things I tried to make whole, mostly people. We can't fix anyone. We're responsible for our own story. Let your family challenge you. And know that the challenge is giving you all opportunities to grow and evolve into the people you're here to become.

The people closest to us show us the way to heal and grow by triggering the old, the unconscious, and the pain. Whatever wounds we have inside will continue to create more of the same triggers in our lives until we've had a chance to heal them. It's part of the genius that is this universe and the intelligence of our souls.

Everything can be traced back to our childhood and moments of trauma and loss we've experienced, large or small. And I learned I'm not my family. I'm not my past. And I want to create a new possibility in a modern, out-of-the-box way.

The beautiful thing about each of our journeys is: Neither blissful moments nor hard-as-fuck moments last forever. That's what makes each and every one of them valuable, precious, and worthy of our complete attention and gratitude. Soak it all in with gratitude.

At the end of the day—it's all love.

Becoming a mother was equally the most terrifying and magical thing I've ever done. I'm learning more about myself and life through watching Cheri and Kai than I'd ever hope to know on my own. Kai, my teacher, is full of timeless wisdom that Cheri shares with me through a wink or gentle touch every single day. Being a mother is hard. Being a human is hard. But that's why we have loved ones to remind us of what matters most—love.

> *"The real source of wealth and capital in this new era is not material things…it is the human mind, the human spirit, the human imagination, and our faith in the future."*
>
> — Steve Forbes

EXERCISE

1. What can you do to heighten humanity's vibration and make the world a better place?

   _____
   _____
   _____

2. Who could use your support with their modern family?

   _____
   _____
   _____

3. What are your dreams for your family, children, and grandchildren?

   _____
   _____
   _____
   _____
   _____
   _____

4. What are your ideas about the future? What will humanity look like?

_____
_____
_____

5. Are you inspired to love more?

_____
_____
_____

FIVE TIPS FOR CREATING YOUR OWN FAMILY LEGACY

1. Live life on your terms.

2. Know your parents' lease on you expired when you turned eighteen.

3. Make your own choices. Love has no boundaries.

4. Surround yourself with people aligned with your ideas and dreams.

5. Understand your legacy is based on your daily actions and kindness.

SUMMARY

We're living in a time when the traditional family doesn't exist anymore. We can all create a family of our own. Family members can be friends. Family has so many forms. Families with gay men and lesbian women raising children. Blended families after divorce and remarrying. Families from different cultures and skin colors. Families with adopted children, surrogate moms, and IVF babies. Families with transgender children and transgenders starting families. And families of our own we created with brothers and sisters from different families.

Family is love. When a family gets started, continues, or changes, love is the foundation. Family and legacy are different for us all. When a family is created out of love, it is a loving family, regardless of the picture. The best legacy we all can leave is loving people more and being less judgmental about what a family should look like. Love is family.

"The greatest gift of family life is to be intimately acquainted with people you might never even introduce yourself to, had life not done it for you."

— Kendall Hailey

CALL TO ACTION

Write all your fears down and burn them. Shout them to the ocean or the mountains. Find a way to release them from your mind and body so you can make peace with your life. Replace that little voice with trust and with love. Running from difficulties because they're challenging is missing out on the greatest learning opportunities. Real life isn't always easy. It's up to you to create the story you want to live and the legacy you want to give to your family. People will judge you no matter what. Love your life. Love your family. Create your story. Create your legacy. Now!

"Family is the most important thing in the world."

— Princess Diana

A Final Note

Become an Empowered Leader

> *"Life is short, that's all there is to say. Get what you can from the present—thoughtfully, justly. Life is short. Do not forget about the most important things in our life, living for other people and doing good for them."*
>
> — Marcus Aurelius

Life is so precious, and I am grateful to be alive. When I grieve, I turn tough moments into something good and try to make the world a little bit better. My loved ones may be gone physically, but a piece of them resides in me, and they would want me to keep moving forward. I will be present and try to get what I want out of life as much as I can—with whatever is in my control—and be at peace with whatever is thrown my way.

We do what we must. Life events are happening for me, not to me. I will be stronger for this and will help people become stronger because of what I've learned. I feel good knowing I can do my part, and I will not regret my life. My hardest moments change me. I become a different person every decade. I choose daily to become better and overcome obstacles and challenges.

I'm committed to sharing my experiences, expertise, wisdom, stories, energy, light, and love with the world. My advice is to choose your self-talk topics and your self-love efforts wisely and to make healing your heart your number-one priority. To create a better world and opportunities for others to grow, learn, and explore what's possible in this lifetime, we need you in your power and your unstoppable drive. Become the example, the mentor, and the hero.

Life is not easy. We experience many phases of growing pains. We all go through them, no exceptions. Work through them, accept them, and move on. As long as you're better today than yesterday, you're leading the way. Nothing happens overnight. Life is a journey. Enjoy it all and become an empowered leader who's impeccable with your words, actions, and love for people.

Become the person you are destined to be. Go through the transformation and become an empowered leader, parent, partner, business owner, friend, employee, sister, brother, child, and cousin. Be an inspiration to your followers who love you for who you are.

About the Author

ESTHER WILDENBERG is an author, professional keynote speaker, accomplished consultant, and sought-after transformation coach.

She is committed to empowering women (and men) while leaving a sustainable legacy today for the next generation. Esther also serves as cofounder and president of Codebreaker Technologies, LLC—the world leader in personality coding technology. With more than two decades of international experience, she understands culture, diversity, inclusion, and the power of team like no other.

After two near-death experiences, Esther's passion is to equip and empower people to manifest their own greatness in business and life. Esther's executive path started at a young age. By age thirty-three, she entered the C-suite, and from there, she held multiple C-suite leadership positions while building her own consulting and coaching company in the Netherlands. In 2014, she moved to the US. Today, her impressive career spans twenty-five years, across multiple industries and continents, yet according to Esther, she's just getting started.

Esther knows how to build companies and personal brands, and most importantly, she knows how to build people into the best, most successful versions of themselves. She's done it countless times throughout her career for the companies she's represented, and now she's called to share her expertise with clients and companies around the world. Esther is a leader's leader who leads from the inside out. Who she is, is how she leads, without exception. Yet her true North Star is her unique grasp of the power of spiritual intelligence and the integrated relationship between us and the world in which we live. Unlike traditional coaches and mentors, Esther has tapped into spiritual intelligence to help businesses and individuals access their deepest values and unlock their greatest purpose to create incredible, real change and drive lasting growth.

The host and facilitator of seventy-five retreats and mastermind groups around the world, Esther has shared the stage with legends and spoken before thousands of people. Her true passion is to help you see the power within you, your true North Star, your divine right and life purpose, your unique skills and talents, and to challenge you to start living life on your terms and become the leader the world needs right now—you!

Esther and her wife Cheri Tree are the parents of a young son, Kai. They live in Southern California.

About Esther Wildenberg's Retreats and Mastermind Gatherings

In addition to her work with Codebreaker Technologies and consulting with Fortune 500 companies and small businesses, Esther has made a name for herself in the realm of personal and professional development. She has successfully hosted seventy-five retreats and mastermind gatherings globally. Her latest endeavor, the ICONIC X mastermind program, targets women entrepreneurs with significant incomes, focusing on mentoring in the eight forms of wealth and the eight intelligences, offering unique travel experiences to inspire and create a lasting impression. She has hosted and facilitated spiritual retreats, transformational retreats, RISE retreats, and leadership retreats. She has empowered masterminds and business accelerators. Thousands have been inspired and transformed by her natural talents and gifts for transforming humans into their highest selves!

ICONIC X Mastermind Program

ICONIC X is an elite opportunity for those dedicated to experiencing life beyond the ordinary. Join Esther Wildenberg and a team of distinguished experts for unparalleled networking and mastermind gatherings, engaging in extraordinary experiences worldwide. This exclusive mastermind group is a sanctuary for those who are passionate about achieving personal and professional greatness and are committed to meaningful growth. Dive into a year of transformation alongside leaders and visionaries on a journey that promises to change your life forever. Your path to an iconic life begins here. This is a twelve-month program, by application only. Your ICONIC Life awaits when you practice all eight forms of wealth in your new lifestyle.

RISE Transformation Retreats

RISE stands for Renew, Inspire, Strengthen, and Evolve. RISE Transformation Retreats are a life-changing experience. They can help you achieve greater personal awareness, equip you to lead a healthier lifestyle, and inspire you to find a greater sense of meaning in your life. If you've suffered from past trauma, a RISE Transformation Retreat can help you heal. If you simply need a chance to unwind and slow down, a RISE Transformation Retreat can provide just that. While it might mean taking a few days off from your regular responsibilities, making time for a transformation retreat is the greatest gift you can give to yourself. Esther's retreats offer the opportunity to embark on a journey of self-discovery and personal growth. Her transformation retreats give you the chance to disconnect from everyday stressors, address physical and emotional blocks, and find a renewed sense of purpose.

> *"Esther Wildenberg is not just an exceptional leadership speaker—she's a true catalyst for empowerment during her retreats and masterminds because they're transformational!"*
>
> — Lisa Thomas, Epigenetics for Global Impact

EMPOWER Masterminds

Esther's Empower Masterminds promote growth mindsets, business ownership, massive income, passive income, and financial freedom! Empower Masterminds are for leaders interested in self-improvement, generational wealth, collaboration, give back initiatives, travel, and enjoying what life has to offer. This mastermind group is designed to support and empower female entrepreneurs in their journey to success and provides a safe and collaborative space for like-minded women to connect, share experiences, gain valuable insights, and grow both personally and professionally.

Empower is a highly focused, action-driven group to support CEOs and business owners seeking to grow their companies through client acquisition, retention, collaboration, and innovation. By participating in the Empower Mastermind, you will become more effective, become a better leader, live a more balanced life, and be healthier. You will free up time on your calendar by becoming more productive and eliminating distractions. Empower is for women across the USA and around the world.

"I've been to five of Esther Wildenberg's Mastermind Retreats. With each retreat, I leave refreshed, invigorated, and restored to go back into my life with energy and clarity to positively influence my family, business, and community. Taking the time to attend Esther's retreats is an investment in myself, which allows me to contribute to others more effectively."

— Teresa Ryan, Century 21

"I have had the honor and pleasure of attending several of Esther Wildenberg's mastermind and training events, including, most recently, an amazing event in Costa Rica. She's a 'mastermind master.' Esther excels in designing her masterminds around deep experience, starting each day with meditation and focusing on positive transformation. She carefully creates content specific to her audience's needs and creates experiential learning through targeted, thought-provoking exercises. As a skilled facilitator, Esther is intuitively attentive to her group's learning and engagement in the content and experience. I look forward to more events with Esther!"

— Laurel Rolls, Certified Executive/Professional Coach ICF

"Retreats with Esther Wildenberg are a game-changer, seamlessly blending powerful information with soulful self-discovery. Having attended several retreats with her, I know you'll discover a transformative experience that unlocks your full potential, offering practical tools and personalized strategies to align your mindset and soul set. Guided by her passion, Esther empowers you to confidently face any challenge. The retreat's holistic approach and supportive community make it a must-attend for those ready to level up their lives and work toward self-mastery."

— Eric Goodman, PhD, Certified Business Coach, Consultant, and Trainer, Meridian Success Group

To learn more or receive an application,
please email: esther@estherwildenberg.com, esther@empaower.com, or text +1 (858) 847-8368.

About Codebreaker Technologies

Esther Wildenberg, cofounder and president of Codebreaker Technologies since 2014, has made significant strides in fostering human connections through the innovative BANK methodology. Alongside her partner and CEO, Cheri Tree, Esther has expanded the application of this method from boosting sales by up to 300 percent to enriching various aspects of human relationships, including education and parenting. BANK is designed to help people make more money in less time. More than 500,000 people have been touched by the BANK system.

Codebreaker Technologies is the world leader in personality coding technology, with clients in fifty countries. Its mission is to connect and empower humanity with their revolutionary tools, training, and technology, powered by BANK. The company is both purpose-driven and profit-driven, and Esther and Cheri are proud to be changing the world every day through the universal language of BANK. Their guiding principle, "Make People Matter," drives their mission to make a positive difference worldwide.

Codebreaker Technologies is powered by BANK, a scientifically validated methodology designed to predict buying and buy-in behavior in nanoseconds. BANK was created in the early 2000s by Founder and Chair Cheri Tree. Her original goal was to find a solution to beat the proverbial numbers game in sales, and ultimately, close more sales in less time. Her system not only revolutionized her income and sales success, but also rapidly expanded globally to top professionals, companies, and industries. Its tagline is "Take it to the BANK."

The launch of Codebreaker Technologies' foundation and the "Make Kids Matter" initiative in January 2024 was a significant step toward their mission. This program aims to provide transformative tools and training to educational and non-profit organizations, matching each purchase with a donation to those who are molding the future.

The world has changed, so the way we do business and connect with others must change as well. We strive every day to serve our clients and make a difference in their lives, personally and professionally. Our goal is to unlock the key to humanity through the universal language of BANK and create "One World, One Language."

"Thanks to Esther Wildenberg, cofounder of Codebreaker Technologies, I went from $265,000 annual income to more than $1,000,000 in gross commissions in six years. Codebreaker Technologies and the BANK system has been a major factor in helping me achieve my sales success. Since taking the course in 2015, I have been able to understand my clients' needs more easily, appreciate my clients' values, and communicate so much more effectively so that people feel understood and heard. This higher emotional intelligence has generated such a high level of trust between me and my clients that they hire me again and again and recommend me to their friends. I know I would not be where I am now without the Codebreaker technology in my sales toolkit."

— Jane Johnston, REMAX, Victoria, British Columbia

ABOUT CODEBREAKER TECHNOLOGIES

"Using BANK with our offshore phone sales team increased conversions from 18 to 32 percent, with an average over the past six months of 25 percent. Our best month secured an extra $63,000,000 in business. That's a 78 percent increase!"

— Carolyn Gibson, Queensland, Australia

"The BANK system allowed me to increase my Airbnb income as a property manager by more than 400 percent. Once I ran my property descriptions and highlights through the AI, I realized I was not speaking to or reaching all the codes. I made some adjustments and started to run my communications and responses to the guests' inquiries and questions through AI and my bookings and sales took off. As a result, we were booked solid from May through September during a time when most Airbnb sites were suffering due to COVID. I am now ranked as one of the top Airbnb hosts in one of the hottest markets in the US thanks to the BANK technology."

— Cathy Compton, Business Owner, Phoenix, Arizona

To learn more, visit the website: www.codebreakertech.com or www.codebreakerglobal.com. For a free consultation, please email esther@codebreakertech.com or text +1 (858) 847-8368.

Engage Esther Wildenberg as a Coach or Consultant

Esther Wildenberg is known by her clients as the "executive whisperer." Esther has been an executive coach and consultant for fifteen years. One of her superpowers is reading people and team dynamics in just minutes. Esther's background includes corporate experience within Fortune 500 companies and small businesses. She has international experience and understands the dynamics of cultural differences, inclusivity, and diversity. Esther is results driven and has impeccable people skills. She will bring a higher level of awareness, spiritual intelligence, EQ, and leadership to your organization.

Esther is committed to serving business leaders and their teams in reaching the highest level of performance and capability. Every business success depends on individual effort, growth, and execution. People are your most important asset, and creating the most optimized A Team is key to a thriving organization.

Esther's executive path started at a young age. By thirty-three, she was the CEO of a financial sales company in Europe, leading a team of 800. From there, she held multiple C-Suite positions while building her own consulting and coaching company in the Netherlands. Today, her impressive career spans twenty years, across multiple industries and continents.

Esther has a direct, no-nonsense approach and her sense of humor makes the journey and transformation fun. She will tell you what you need to hear, not what you want to hear. Her goal is to ensure systemic implementation using unique tools and accountability to get results fast. As she says: "I'm not here to stay."

Whether you're an individual looking to unlock your full potential, an executive who wants to bring out the best in your team, or a business owner who wants to drive growth and change in your business, you've come to the right place. Esther Wildenberg will transform you, your teams, and your business beyond what you thought possible.

"I retained Esther Wildenberg as a coach for our leadership team at the Marquette Companies. She is a very experienced coach and does a very effective job of finding the challenges to be faced and addressing them in a very succinct way. I highly recommend Esther to anyone who wants to take their team to the next level."

— Nick Ryan, Executive Chairman, Marquette Companies

"Esther is a very pleasant, professional person to work with and is focused on delivering results."

— Michael van Den Berg, Head of Audit, Shell Global

"I met Esther in a dynamic phase in a changing organization. She has the ability to combine creative thoughts with a results-driven approach. As a business consultant, she perfectly keeps the balance between the interests of businesses and individuals. What most struck me is her never-ceasing positivism, making her always capable of finding a solution and seeing the sunny side!"

— Annet Luijendijk, Executive Consultant ING

ENGAGE ESTHER WILDENBERG AS A CONSULTANT

Inspired to book a free consultation? Please email esther@estherwildenberg.com, esther@empaower.com, or text +1 (858) 847-8368.

Book Esther Wildenberg to Speak at Your Next Event

Esther is a seasoned speaker with a true passion for transforming people's lives and inspiring them to live their best possible life. Esther has a very direct and funny way of sharing her message. She will move you in many ways, and you will act after you hear her speak. She leaves no room for excuses. She's passionate about her two favorite topics: Worldclass Leadership and Spiritual Intelligence in Business.

Spiritual Intelligence is the future. Not many people touch this topic because it often gets confused with religion. Spiritual intelligence is not religion! It's your true North Star, your why, your natural talents, gifts, and reason you're here on earth.

Esther's spiritual connection is behind every ounce of her success. Her spiritual connection began when:

1. *Purpose and calling* revealed her truth.

2. *Confidence* allowed her to heal within and release her limiting beliefs.

3. *Innovation* allowed her to develop her ability to focus on solutions instead of problems.

4. Collaboration combined with her higher consciousness brought extraordinary people into her life automatically.

Worldclass leadership is not about power, titles, rank, or income. Leadership is who you are and the example you set every day. Esther has trained others in companies where managers were better leaders than in the C-suite! Your true power shows when you live your true gifts, talents, and values—when you really care about people and have high EQ.

Esther will dive deeply into your layers of disappointment, fear, perfectionism, pain, rejection, and insecurity to show you what your superpowers are. World-class leaders focus on mastery, creativity, authenticity, vulnerability, teamwork, and humanity. When you transition from fame and fortune into authentic leadership, you will be a world-class leader. You're responsible for how you present yourself as a leader. It's your journey; it's up to you to become the best leader possible. That's were true success lays.

"Esther is a speaker who will light the fire of inspiration and challenge you to commit to change. She does not dance around the challenges we all face on our success journey, and her honesty is what allows people to take steps forward."

— Jaime Taets, CEO of Keystone Group International

"Esther, you are an extraordinarily gifted and inspirational speaker. Your level of connection and clarity with the audience brought back memories of Walter Cronkite and Walt Disney. Thank you for your contribution to our leadership event. You created a buzz!"

— Nick Ryan, Executive Chairman, Marquette Companies

BOOK ESTHER WILDENBERG TO SPEAK AT ...

To book Esther as a speaker, please email esther@estherwildenberg.com, esther@empaower.com, or esther@codebreakertech.com, or text +1 (858) 847-8368.

www.ingramcontent.com/pod-product-compliance
Lightning Source LLC
Chambersburg PA
CBHW052113200426
43209CB00057B/1604